COMPREHENSION QUARTERLY

# CQ

**ISSUE A:** Inferring

# ON THE EDGE OF YOUR SEAT

# On the Edge of Your Seat
## THINK ABOUT: Inferring

**A4**

NONFICTION
### That Sinking Feeling
Beware! Is the ground beneath you really solid?

PUBLIC ALERT!

Ground may sink or release toxic

**A11**

FICTION
### Danger Lurks Underground
Discover why people are packing up and leaving town.

**A19**

FICTION
### Cody's Call to Danger
Find out what happens when a Bear Dog meets a mother grizzly.

**A25**

NONFICTION
### Lights, Camera, Suspense!
Learn how filmmakers create suspense in movies.

## In this issue:

## INFERRING

# Let's Go to the Movies

Isabel loves to go to movies, and this Friday night her dad has promised to drive her and her friend Charise to the local movie theater, the Carousel 12. But which of the 12 movies should the girls see? Isabel looks up the short reviews in the movie section of Friday's paper. She notes that six of the films at the theater seem to be for grown-ups, so she scratches those off her list. Three of the films for families and children have a one-star rating. And since Isabel knows the movies are rated no stars (terrible) to four stars (great), she uses the strategy of **inferring** to decide that those three movies are probably not worth seeing. Here are the reviews of the three remaining films.

★★★↘ *Great Grizzlies!* Bud Baxter stars in an exciting adventure story about a young man who saves a grizzly cub from hunters. Baxter gives the performance of his career. 95 minutes.

★★★ *Marchmont School Madness* The wacky and wildly popular duo of Melanie and Harvey are back in another installment of the Marchmont School saga. Kids just keep coming back for more of these! 115 minutes.

★★ *Bowling Beagles* Beagles that bowl? It can't be, but it is, in this fantasy by legendary animator Sheldon Clinghoffer. The bold bowling team of beagles will keep you on the edge of your seat as they bowl their way to fame. 105 minutes.

Isabel calls her friend, and the two girls discuss the reviews and make some inferences based on them. They infer that *Great Grizzlies!* and *Bowling Beagles* are probably similar to some movies they saw recently; however, the girls have seen all the other Marchmont School movies and really loved them. So it's no contest. They choose *Marchmont School Madness.*

Think about some of the movies you have seen or books you have read lately. What inferences did you make that helped you decide which movies or books to choose?

# That SINKING FEELING

by Maureen Mecozzi

**D**o you know the expression *rock solid?* It means something that's dependable and reliable, something as firm as the ground you walk on.

In most places, ground is the most rock-solid thing around. But in some parts of the United States and in several other countries, the ground is a lot less solid than it appears. Without warning, a hole can open up in a field, a backyard, or a street. Whatever is on the surface—houses, cars, a basketball court—sinks down below.

Some sinkholes occur naturally in geologic formations called *karsts*. Others are the accidental result of human actions. In areas with abandoned coal mines, sinkholes often occur when old tunnels crumble and collapse. Both kinds of sinkholes are dangerous for anyone or anything on the surface.

Sinkholes can open up in the ground without any warning.

# Narrow Escape from a BURNING HOLE

The small mining town of Centralia lies in the heart of eastern Pennsylvania's coal country. Coal is a valuable natural fuel. It's difficult to **ignite,** but once it starts burning, it gives off plenty of heat and burns slowly and steadily.

Since the 1850s, Centralia's miners had been digging deep tunnels below ground to get the coal and bring it to the surface. As they dug, the miners supported the tunnel roofs and walls with wooden beams. When a mine no longer produced enough coal, it was abandoned, and the miners would dig another mine.

The web of mines and tunnels grew over time as more and more coal was brought to the surface. Centralia grew, too—houses, schools, shops, and churches were built right on top of the abandoned mines.

In 1962, burning trash in an open pit near a mine started a fire in the tunnels below. The fire spread easily as the remaining coal and old wood beams burned on and on. Firefighters tried to put out the fire, but this was like stopping a fire-breathing dragon. The years wore on and still the fire burned.

People in Centralia began noticing some strange things about their town. The air smelled like rotten eggs, and poisonous gases drifted up through the soil and into homes. People felt tired and many became ill. Roads and sidewalks cracked and caved in. Buildings moved and fell down as the soil shifted and resettled. Smoke and steam rose up from the ground, and the soil was hot to the touch.

Then, on February 14, 1981, twelve-year-old Todd Domboski bent down to look at a small fire in a pile of leaves in his grandmother's backyard. Suddenly, the ground beneath him collapsed, and a hot, foul-smelling smoking hole about four feet wide opened up. Steam hissed all around him as he sank deeper and deeper into the hole. Todd grabbed a tree root and held on as the size of the hole increased to a depth of 150 feet. Huge flames snapped at his legs.

Sinkholes can be 150 feet deep.

A cousin saw Todd's red cap through the smoke and pulled him to safety. Had Todd sunk any deeper, the heat or the poisonous gases would have killed him instantly.

The sinkhole that almost swallowed Todd appeared because an old tunnel had collapsed. The underground fire had burned away the tunnel's old supporting timbers. Because of Todd's experience and all the other problems Centralia was having because of the fire, many people moved away.

> How would putting out the fire in the tunnels be like stopping a fire-breathing dragon?

# CENTRALIA

Steam rises from cracks in the ground.

The Centralia fire is still burning today, more than 40 years after it started! It can't be put out like an ordinary fire. Water poured into old tunnels usually just seeps away, as it would if you poured a glass of water on the ground. Sometimes the water changes to steam, which creates pressure and can cause an explosion. Firefighters try to cut off the supply of oxygen by tightly closing entrances, but mines have many cracks that allow oxygen in. And with so much uncovered coal below, this fire has plenty of fuel.

The hope was, and is, that someday the fire might burn itself out. Meanwhile, the old tunnels cave in and new sinkholes continue to pull down trees, houses, and roads. But few people are around to notice. At one time, 1,100 people lived in Centralia. Today, only about 20 people live there.

Would you want to live in Centralia? Why or why not?

A road is closed because of a sinkhole.

The fire continues to burn.

One rowhouse remains standing.

# Without Adequate Support,
# YOU SINK!

In the summer of 1999, the Tholen family of Everett, Washington, had sunk plenty of money and time into fixing up a classic sports car. Imagine how unhappy they were when a 60-foot-deep sinkhole opened wide, taking down the car and an 80-foot Japanese maple tree in their backyard!

In April 2000, in Shelby, North Carolina, Louie Hudson was enjoying a meal with friends at a restaurant. He looked out the window to see the front end of his luxury car tipping slowly into a big hole. It took a tow truck with a **winch** a half-hour to pull Mr. Hudson's wheels to solid ground.

> How do you think you would feel if your car was tipping into a big hole?

The students at a junior high school in Jefferson County, Alabama, learned about sinkholes firsthand during a field trip held on school grounds. Parts of their school cafeteria began **subsiding** in the spring of 2000, and the problem continued throughout the summer in some classrooms and bathrooms.

These are just a few of the many sinkhole **sagas** that are reported in newspapers all around the U.S., especially in the summer months. What's going on?

Call it an unfortunate combination of climate, natural **topography**, and human activity. In certain parts of the country, the topmost layers of the earth are made of rocks that have a lot of cracks, or **fissures**. Sometimes large **caverns** form between the rock layers. This is called "karst terrain."

Normally, **groundwater** fills the cracks and caverns and helps the rock layers stay firm and solid. When there's a **drought**, however, the level of water in the ground drops lower and lower. The soil up above begins to slip and slide into the cracks and other openings in the rock, and that's when sinkholes appear. If there happens to be a big cavern below, look out!

Sinkholes can occur even if there's not a drought. When people pump too much water from wells or tackle large construction projects like highways and subdivisions that interrupt the flow of water through the ground, the same thing happens. Without enough water to fill the cracks, the rock

Hewitt-Trussville Junior High School

becomes unstable. Whatever is built on top may take a fall into a sinkhole.

It would seem the answer to a sinkhole is simple: Just get a big shovel and fill it up with dirt or cement! That works for some of the tiny holes. For the big ones—there are sinkholes hundreds of feet wide and a hundred or more feet deep—it's not a practical or economical solution. Sometimes the only answer is to move homes, businesses, and roads to more solid, safer ground.

We can't stop all sinkholes, but we can be more aware of the ground we walk on. Understanding the **geology** of the places where we live can guide us as we build our neighborhoods and towns. ◉

What do you understand now about sinkholes that you didn't understand before?

The road is closed due to a giant sinkhole.

Places where coal mine fires continue to burn are called hot spots.

# Glossary

**caverns** – large underground caves

**drought** – a long period of time with no rain

**fissures** – narrow cracks in a rock layer

**geology** – the study of the structure of the earth

**groundwater** – water beneath the earth's surface

**ignite** – to set fire to and cause to burn

**saga** – a long story

**subside** – to sink to a lower level

**topography** – the physical features of a place

**winch** – a hand-powered or machine-powered drum around which a cable winds as a load is lifted

# Stop and Respond

## SINKHOLE MAP

Sinkholes occur in many parts of the world. Make a list of the locations of the sinkholes described in the article. With a friend, locate the places on a map.

## PUT IT OUT!

List ways to put out a fire. Then use this list to infer a new method to put out the Centralia fire. Make a diagram of your new plan and use labels to explain it.

## POSTCARD FROM CENTRALIA

You've just visited Centralia and are looking for a postcard to send to your best friend back home. You're unable to find a postcard showing exactly what you want. You decide to make your own and show what you infer to be the most important Centralia scene. Draw a picture showing this scene.

# Believe It or Not!

Have you ever been in a situation when your heart beat unusually fast? Have you ever had a "rush" of unexpected strength that helped you do something you didn't think you could do? Read on to find out about one such extraordinary happening.

When Arnold Learner was fifty years old, he had a heart attack. Because of the damage caused to his heart, he did not lift heavy objects.

Six years after his heart attack, Learner was taking a walk when he heard a cry for help. He ran to the playground and found a five-year-old boy trapped under a heavy cast iron pipe. Learner quickly lifted the pipe and saved the child's life.

Learner said that at the time he had thought the pipe weighed between 300 and 400 pounds. It actually weighed 1,800 pounds—almost a ton! Several days later, Learner, his two grown sons, a newspaper reporter, and a policeman returned to the playground and tried to lift the pipe. None of them could!

There are many documented stories similar to this one. The answer to how a person can perform super-human feats is found in your body's response to anger, stress, or frightening situations.

When your mind identifies a serious threat, your body has an automatic alarm that lets you use the full power of all your resources to eliminate the danger. Your nervous system fires rapidly and releases hormones, such as adrenaline. This is called the fight-or-flight reaction because these changes get the body ready to do battle or to run away. Adrenaline causes your heart to beat faster and stronger. This raises your blood pressure. If a large amount of adrenaline is released, an ordinary person can gain the strength to do an extraordinary feat.

# DANGER
## LURKS UNDERGROUND
### by Mike Graf

"Pass the shovel, Tim," Erica directed her brother.

Tim handed a small plastic shovel to his younger sister and went back to building a tiny stick house. He snapped twigs in half and set them on a square frame of larger twigs. Then he set pieces of bark on top for the roof. "I'm done with our house," he said as he moved aside. "Can you make our road next?"

"Sure." Erica moved over to where Tim had been and pushed the shovel smoothly through the sand between the houses. "There!" Erica remarked as she sat back to look at the miniature model of their town, Centerville.

Tim grabbed a stick and traced a large circle in the sand near the edge of town.

"What's that?" Erica asked.

"The abandoned coal plant," Tim answered.

Tim flung the stick aside and started digging with his hands around one of the twig houses near the coal plant until the house fell apart. He pulled a toy fire engine from his pocket and drove it along the road toward the collapsed house.

"Another house has collapsed because of the underground coal fire," Tim announced in a deep voice.

Erica grabbed a bucket from the sandbox and ran over to the faucet. She filled the bucket, walked back, and poured the water over the imaginary fire.

"Fire's out!" Tim announced.

"I wish it were that easy," a man's voice surprised Tim and Erica. They turned around, stood up, and squinted into the sunshine. Standing at the edge of their backyard sandbox was their father dressed in a fire-fighting uniform and holding a heavy helmet. Clipped to his belt was a handi-talkie unit, or HTU, with voices crackling on and off.

"Hi, Dad!" both Tim and Erica shouted.

"Hi, kids!" Mr. Parker answered. He turned down the volume on his HTU. "It's too bad we can't use water to put out real coal fires."

Erica looked back at the wet sand. "Why not?"

"If water gets underground, the burning coal turns it to steam," their father explained, "and then there could be an explosion."

What does putting out a fire mean to you? Is it an easy or hard thing to do? Why do you think that?

"So, how do you put out coal fires?" Tim asked.

"I wish I knew," their father answered. "It's hard to put out a fire you can't see. We've tried smothering the fire, building firebreaks, and digging out the burning coal. Nothing's worked. And everything we try is expensive." He looked down at the sandbox. "Hey, what's all this?"

"Our town," Tim responded.

They squatted down and Mr. Parker set his helmet on the edge of the sandbox. He and his children quietly looked around at the model of their nearly deserted town.

Finally, Mr. Parker spoke. "Back in the old days, this town had several thousand people. But, now almost everyone has left. Even the public library is gone." He shook his head and slowly stood up. "Come on, kids. Let's go get lunch." He hoisted Erica onto his shoulders and extended a hand to Tim.

As they headed inside, Erica blurted out, "I don't want to move."

"Me neither," Tim agreed.

"We'll do whatever we can to stay." Mr. Parker pushed the kitchen door open and announced to his wife, "We're home, Susan!"

After lunch, Tim jumped out of his chair. "Come on, Erica, I have an idea." The children disappeared into Tim's room and soon returned carrying a shoe box.

"Erica and I are on a mission to raise money to help put out the coal mine fire," Tim proclaimed. He set the box on the table.

"This is our collection box!" Erica declared proudly.

"Hmm . . . it costs a lot of money to put out coal fires," Mr. Parker replied. "But, you know, we can use all the help we can get." He smiled at his children, reached into his pocket for a handful of coins, and dropped them into the shoe box.

A voice suddenly reported over the HTU, "Ryan Parker? This is dispatch."

"Yes, go ahead, Trevor," Mr. Parker answered.

"Can you check on the dead trees near the old mine on Coal Street? Someone just called in saying the area around the dead trees is more smoky than normal."

"I'm on my way," Mr. Parker responded. He grabbed his helmet from the kitchen counter and said to his wife, "I'll see you all at supper."

Tim lifted the shoe box from the table. "Come on, Erica, let's go."

"Where do you think you two are going?" their mother asked.

"To collect money!" Tim replied. "Can we?"

"Well, OK," Mrs. Parker agreed hesitantly, "but stay on our street."

Tim and Erica ran to the Scott's house next door and rang the doorbell. Slowly the door creaked open.

"Tim! Erica!" Mrs. Scott greeted them warmly.

Mr. Scott appeared from behind his wife, carrying a CB scanner, and grumbled, "What have you kids got there?"

Tim gulped, "We're raising money to help put out the underground coal fire so we don't have to move." He held up the shoe box and shook it so the coins clinked together.

"It won't do you any good," Mr. Scott muttered grumpily. "I tried to stop that fire when I worked for the fire department forty years ago. And it's still burning!"

Suddenly, a message came over Mr. Scott's scanner. "Ryan Parker has reported a massive sinkhole collapsing at the end of Coal Street. All units respond immediately! This is an emergency!"

"Daddy!" Erica shouted.

The voice on the scanner continued, "We've just lost contact with Parker!"

The children bolted off the porch, leaving their shoe box behind.

Erica and Tim ran to Coal Street and found their father's empty truck. They stopped to catch their breath in front of a warning sign.

Why do you think Erica and Tim left the Scott's so quickly?

Surrounding them were broken fences and empty lots where houses used to be. Cracked and uneven sidewalks lead to nowhere, and the street was filled with potholes. Far in the distance was a grove of dead trees.

"There!" Tim roared. "That's where Dad should be!"

The children hurried in the direction of the trees. Steam and smoke rose from the parched ground, and the air smelled like rotten eggs. Tim called out, "Hold your shirt over your mouth and nose, Erica."

They ran on until they came to the edge of an immense volcanic-looking sinkhole with billowing smoke. About 50 feet below, a bed of glowing orange embers burned and crackled like hot coals in a campfire. Tim felt a wave of heat against his face and grabbed Erica's hand, pulling her back from the edge.

Tim fanned his hand in front of his eyes and peered through the thick smoke, looking for his father. He briefly caught sight of someone clinging to a tree on the other side of the collapsing cauldron.

"There's Dad!" Tim screamed. "Come on, Erica!" The children dashed around the edge of the sinkhole. As Tim ran, he stepped on a loose piece of sidewalk that started slipping into the hole. He jumped to the side and watched the concrete fall into the pit.

The smoke cleared again. For a second they could see the far side of the pit. Dangling into the hole was their father, his arms stretched upward and his hands grasping two large tree roots.

"Dad!" Tim yelled. He and Erica ran toward their father.

Suddenly, the ground started shaking as if there were an earthquake.

"Ahh!" their father cried out. The children froze in horror. One of the tree's roots had snapped off, and their father now hung above the fire pit by one arm. Tim and Erica watched silently, holding their breath. Their father struggled to get a foothold on the crumbling cliff, but loose dirt gave way and tumbled into the deep abyss. Finally, he was able to swing his other arm around and grab the root so he hung by both arms.

"Daddy!" Erica screamed. She and Tim crept closer.

Their father looked helplessly at his children and shook his head. He exclaimed hoarsely, "No, kids! Get back!"

> What do you think would cause the ground to shake? How might this effect Mr. Parker?

The children stepped away from the edge. The fire sizzled below, and the ground felt hot under their feet.

"Go get help!" Mr. Parker called out. The ground began shaking again, and their father grunted loudly as he clawed his way up the tree until both his arms were wrapped around the trunk. His feet rested on the root where his hands had been. More ground broke away under the tree, but it somehow remained anchored in place.

Sirens sounded back where the truck was parked. The ground shook again and the tree cracked sharply and began tearing away from the edge. Without thinking, Tim ran toward his father. At the same time, his father desperately lunged upward, grabbed hold of the ground behind the tree, and frantically kicked his feet up the dirt wall until he was able to rest his stomach on the edge. Tim reached his father and bent down and tugged him away from the hole. In one swift motion, his father got to his feet, scooped up Tim, and ran toward Erica, just as the tree tipped slowly over and plunged into the fiery pit.

Three firefighters appeared out of the thick smoke. One shouted, "Ryan! Are you OK?"

"Yes! We're getting out of here!" Mr. Parker called back. He lifted Erica onto his other arm and ran to his truck. After helping his children in, he climbed into the driver's seat and started the engine.

When he was a safe distance from the sinkhole, Mr. Parker pulled over to the side of the road. He slumped forward and rested his head on the steering wheel.

"Dad?" Tim whispered. "Are you OK?"

"I was thinking just now," Mr. Parker sighed. He turned his head and looked at Tim, then Erica. "We need to go home and start packing."

What do you think Mr. Parker means when he says that they need to go home and start packing? Why would he say this?

# Stop and Respond

## Make This Film!

Pretend that you've been asked to persuade a film studio to make a movie based on "Danger Lurks Underground." List five reasons why you think this story would make a good movie.

## Pros and Cons

By the end of the story, Mr. Parker makes the decision that the family should move from Centerville. What are some of the reasons for his decision? What are some reasons some people might choose to stay? Use your inferring skills and make a two-column chart that lists reasons to remain and reasons to leave Centerville.

## The ABCs of a Sinkhole

With a partner, create an alphabet poem about the Centerville sinkhole. For each letter of the alphabet, think of a word that describes or relates to the sinkhole. Present your poem to the class and tell about the words you chose.

**INFERRING**

# So, What Did You Think?

*Marchmont School Madness* and the other Marchmont School movies were adapted from a series of novels about Marchmont School. As fans of the series, Isabel and Charise have read and enjoyed many of the books. So they were especially interested to see the movie *Marchmont School Madness* because they had not read the book yet.

When the movie was over, Isabel and Charise bought soft drinks and waited in the lobby for Isabel's father to pick them up. "What did you think?" Charise asked Isabel.

Isabel thought for a moment and then answered, "I liked the movie a lot. It was funny and exciting, and the acting was great. Now I really want to read the book. It's got to be as good as the movie! In fact, I'm going to buy the book and read it right away."

As Isabel read the book, she couldn't help but compare it with the movie. She noticed how the episode in the book, where Mrs. Lumpkin's big Saint Bernard, Atlas, pulled a frantic Mrs. Lumpkin out of the quicksand, was not included in the movie. She also noticed that several of the book's characters were not included in the movie. After Isabel completed the book and she thought about all the things that were not in the movie, she used the strategy of **inferring** to conclude that the book was much better than the movie.

Think about a book that you've read that was made into a movie. What inferences did you make to determine which was better — the book or the movie?

# Bear Dogs:

## Profiles in Bravery

Teams of Karelian Bear Dogs are helping to deal with problem bears who wander into places populated with people, such as towns and campgrounds. The Bear Dogs have been trained to drive black and grizzly bears away from places that they shouldn't be. Meet these brave dogs and find out about their special qualities and skills.

Name: **Carmen**
Sex: **Female**
Birthday: **February 15**
Weight: **58 lbs.**
Special Skills: **loves to bark, great tracker**
Personality: **gentle, loving, mellow**

Name: **Rio**
Sex: **Male**
Birthday: **August 19**
Weight: **60 lbs.**
Special Skills: **best ground tracker, outstanding at finding improperly stored foods in campgrounds**
Personality: **light-hearted, loves people**

Name: **Tuffy**
Sex: **Male**
Birthday: **January 25**
Weight: **46 lbs.**
Special Skills: **lead dog, fastest dog, best barker**
Personality: **serious but loves to play, extremely independent**

Name: **Eilu**
Sex: **Female**
Birthday: **August 14**
Weight: **52 lbs**
Special Skills: **loves to hunt and track bears, good at treeing bears, unbelievably good nose**
Personality: **very intelligent, sensitive, quite a talker**

# Cody's Call to Danger

## by Susan Meyers

The bear was a grizzly. I was sure of it, even though I hadn't yet seen it. Cody was, too. He strained at his leash, barking furiously. The fur on his back bristled. Every muscle in his body seemed to quiver. He never acted this way around black bears. With them he was forceful, but businesslike. "Just doing my job" was his attitude as we worked to warn bears away from cabins, campgrounds, and trails.

With grizzlies it was different. The scent of the huge, silver-coated animals seemed to touch something deep in his being. It was as if he were carried back a thousand years or more, to the days when his Bear Dog ancestors hunted in the remote northern forests of Finland and Russia. Cody and I had worked together here in the Montana wilderness for nearly two years, but seeing him like this made me realize there was a part of him I'd never really know.

"Good boy, good boy," I said, stroking his shiny black-and-white coat.

I knelt down and fitted my hand into one of the footprints the bear had left in the soft earth around the overturned garbage cans. It was at least twelve inches long. The claws that had dug deeply into the earth as the bear feasted on corncobs, chicken bones, and stale sweet rolls added another three inches. Only a grizzly could have left tracks that size.

How would grizzly tracks be like tracks you've seen? How would they be different?

There were lots of smaller tracks, too. Cody sniffed at them eagerly. Cubs! My heart sank as I realized what we were up against—a protective mother grizzly teaching her youngsters how to find an easy meal in a campground filled with careless campers. I was glad that the rest of my team of dogs and handlers would be here before nightfall. It usually takes three barking dogs and their handlers, sometimes firing rounds of beanbags or rubber bullets, to move a bear and cure its desire to enter campgrounds and trails. Having to face a grizzly and her cubs with just one dog, even a great one like Cody, was not something I wanted to do.

Do you think a mother grizzly acts differently toward her cub than other animal mothers act toward their young? Why or why not?

"Hey!" A voice suddenly broke into my thoughts. I turned to see a young boy and girl watching me.

"Are you the bear lady?" the girl asked curiously.

Cody gave up the bear tracks and wagged his tail. He loves kids. Sometimes I think he feels as strongly about them as he does about bears. He looked up at me hopefully, waiting for permission to greet the children.

"Yes, I am," I replied. "I'm Cathy Kelly and this is Cody. He's a Karelian Bear Dog. He comes from Karelia, a region between Finland and Russia. He's specially trained to herd bears out of campgrounds like this one. Would you like to meet him?"

The children's faces lit up. They stepped forward eagerly. "We heard you were coming," the girl said as Cody held out his paw to shake hands. "They said a bear was here last night. I wish I'd seen it."

"Me too," said the boy. "I like bears. If I saw one, I'd give it this." He pulled a partially eaten piece of beef jerky out of his pocket.

"I'm afraid that wouldn't be a good idea," I said. "Bears may look friendly, but they can be dangerous if they come to get food from you. When you're camping in bear country you have to store all your food in bear-proof containers. And no eating popcorn and s'mores in your tent!"

"Oh, I wouldn't do that," said the girl. The boy tucked the beef jerky back in his pocket, a guilty look on his face.

"Good," I said. "Now you'd better get back to your campsite. It'll be dark soon. And don't worry about those bears. They won't stay around long with three Karelians barking at them."

Famous last words . . . That's what I thought a few hours later as I hung up the telephone in the ranger's cabin. The conversation had been brief. The dogs weren't coming. The truck had broken down. "We won't be able to get there until tomorrow," my partner said. "You and Cody better lay low tonight. It's not worth taking chances with a grizzly."

I knew he was right. I was glad that the ranger and I had spent the last few hours warning campers about storing their food securely and staying close to their campsites. The garbage cans had been emptied and the area had been cleaned. With any luck, the bears wouldn't bother to return.

"I'd better walk you back to your truck," said the ranger. He handed me a flashlight and took a rifle from a rack on the wall. "Just in case," he assured me.

"I hope you won't have to use it." The idea of shooting a grizzly, even to save my own life, disturbed me. There were only a thousand or so left in the lower 48 states. I was supposed to be saving them by teaching them to stay away from people. I'd hate to see one destroyed because I hadn't been able to do my job.

Why would it be better not to shoot a grizzly?

Cody's ears perked up as we started out across the dark campground. As we walked, I shined the flashlight into the surrounding trees and bushes, keeping a sharp eye out for a shape that might be a bear.

Suddenly, Cody, who'd been trotting ahead of me at the end of his lead, froze. Initially, a low rumbling sound escaped from his throat. Behind me I heard the ranger get his rifle ready as something moved into the light. My muscles tensed. Then I realized it wasn't a bear. It was the young boy I'd met earlier in

the day. His eyes were open and he was walking, but he seemed not to see us, not to see anything, in fact. A sleepwalker! I recognized the signs. My brother used to do it all the time.

Cody stepped toward the boy. I expected to see his tail start wagging. Instead, the rumbling in his throat became a growl as a huge silver-coated grizzly suddenly appeared from the bushes. Her head swayed from side to side. She sniffed deeply, moving forward as if drawn by some appealing smell. A pair of cubs followed at her heels.

I felt my body tense. A sickening feeling came over me as a vision of the boy stuffing the beef jerky into his pants pocket came to mind. Had they been gray sweatpants, the very same gray sweatpants he was wearing now?

I caught my breath as Cody exploded in a volley of barks. He leaped forward, nearly pulling me off my feet. I let go of the leash. Cody charged at the bear. With deep concentration, I raced for the boy. In a second I had him in my arms.

From the bushes where Cody had chased the bear and her cubs, I heard snarling, scuffling, and then a high-pitched yelp. With his spirit and courage Cody would never back down. Was he tangled by his leash? My heart sank.

Where have you heard snarling and scuffling sounds? How would the sounds in the bushes be like or different from those sounds?

I thrust the now wide-awake boy into the ranger's arms. With no thought of my own safety, I plunged into the bushes. I wasn't going to let my best friend get hurt. I was ready to fight with my bare hands if necessary, but even before my eyes had adjusted to the darkness, the mother bear and her cubs ran out from the other side of the bushes. They tore off, heading for the hills beyond the camp. Cody started after them, but I stopped him with a frantic shout.

"Cody! Leave it! Let them go!"

He turned and came prancing back to my open arms. Fighting back tears, I knelt and ran my hands over his body.

"Is he OK?" cried the boy, as he and the ranger rushed to my side.

"Yes," I said. Cody's tail began to thump against the ground. He reached up to lick my face, his mouth open in a big, panting smile. He was so proud of himself— he knew he'd done his job.

"May I give Cody this?" the boy asked. He pulled the half-eaten piece of beef jerky out of his pocket.

I looked at the ranger. We both knew we should deliver a lecture. Later on we would, but neither of us had the heart for it now. "Sure," I said, stroking Cody's beautiful head. "He deserves it!"  ◯

How is the Karelian Bear Dog, Cody, like other dogs you know? How is he different?

# Stop and Respond

## PROFILE OF A STAR

Does the story, "Cody's Call to Danger," have what it takes to be made into a movie? Could Cody become a Hollywood canine movie star? Make some inferences as to how Cody is just like or different from other animals you've seen in movies or on TV. Then write a profile of Cody, the canine movie star.

## CODY THE BEAR DOG

From reading the story, "Cody's Call to Danger," what special qualities do you infer Karelian Bear Dogs have? Use a two-column chart. In one column, list three words that you think describe a Bear Dog's special qualities. In the other column, write examples you find in the story that demonstrate these qualities.

| Bear Dog qualities | Examples from Story |
|---|---|
| 1 | 1 |
| 2 | 2 |
| 3 | 3 |

## WHAT WAS THAT?

Put yourself in a grizzly's place. You're nosing around the same garbage dump you always visit, when suddenly, a team of dogs comes running straight at you barking ferociously. What do you do? Create a comic strip about an encounter with Karelian Bear Dogs told from a grizzly's point of view.

# LIGHTS, CAMERA, SUSPENSE!

## BY ELAINE ISRAEL

**You're in a theater. Up on the screen is a scene so suspenseful that you're sitting on the edge of your seat. Which of these scenes are you watching?**

- Walking down a deserted street, the heroine suddenly hears footsteps. Curious, she slowly turns. She sees . . . no one.

- Two people are lost in the deep woods on a stormy night.

- A creature with long teeth, claws, and one large eye in the middle of its forehead seems to jump off the screen into your lap.

- Under a full moon, a hound howls. Doors creak. Floors squeak.

**These situations may cause any of us to break out in goose bumps. They're all make-believe, but each is a much-used device to create suspense.**

# MAKEUP TRICKERY

Computers help produce many a chill: a twisting tornado chases down a young couple, a hungry fish seeks a human snack, a terrifying monster smashes a building with its tail. But the scariest effects of all are still made by humans.

Movie makeup artists can transform actors into monsters or alien creatures. They can make a twenty-year-old person look like he or she is eighty years old or make actors appear as if they have been in horrible accidents. Well-done movie makeup can make grown people scream, even though they know that the facial features of the scariest creatures are the work of these talented makeup artists.

One of the first makeup artists was actor Lon Chaney, Sr. He was called the "man of a thousand faces" and appeared in more than 150 roles between 1913 and 1930. For the different characters he played, he emphasized his facial features by using many different materials, such as fish skin, mortician's wax, and grease paint.

Latex, a type of rubber that dries quickly and stays flexible, is often used today to create skin. Makeup artists can apply the latex in thin coats directly to the actor's body. However, each layer must dry before another layer is added. This can be time-consuming. For some movies, actors can be in the makeup room eight hours before each day's filming!

What have you done that is time-consuming? How is applying makeup on actors like that?

# BUILDING SUSPENSE

You don't need blood and gore to make audiences bite their nails and need a manicure. Sound effects and music do the trick as well, or even better. And, believe it or not, some of the scariest films weren't even made in color. A black-and-white

**Lon Chaney, Sr. and his son Lon Chaney, Jr. were transformed by makeup.**

movie, with its shadings and shadows, can leave you on the edge of your seat—even when nothing is about to happen.

Your shudders are real as the star looks nervously into a thick fog, running away from the muffled footsteps of someone she can't see. The stronger your imagination, the scarier the scene. That's because your mind is filling in what isn't shown.

It doesn't spoil the suspense to know that some actions, like the footsteps, were actually created miles away in a sound studio. A person wearing heavy boots was recorded walking away from a microphone on a concrete floor. The smoky fog seemed so real. Who cares that it comes from a machine? And that the poor, threatened actress, who seemed to be so alone, was actually surrounded by a director, assistants, camera operators, and a cast of dozens on a crowded set.

Imagine the fear an audience experiences whenever a certain piece of symphonic music plays—the steady beat-beat-beat of a drum, the soft scratch of a violin, the dum-de-dum-dum-dum of the orchestra. Something, or someone, unfriendly hides nearby. The actor hasn't got a clue; he can't hear the music. But you do; you can. And you are afraid, very afraid. You know the window slapping open and shut, open and shut, and the partially opened door in an empty house are warnings. A nasty event is about to happen.

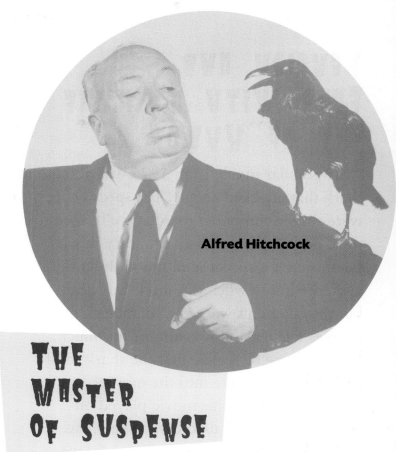

**Alfred Hitchcock**

# THE MASTER OF SUSPENSE

The more involved the audience, the more suspenseful the movie. Alfred Hitchcock directed some of the best mystery movies ever made and is an inspiration to many filmmakers. He said that an audience must believe it is part of the movie. He insisted that no one be allowed to enter the theater once one of his movies had started. He wanted people to see the movie from beginning to end.

Hitchcock explained that the audience likes to think they are one step ahead of the plot. They like to predict what will happen. So Hitchcock fooled them. The twists and turns of his stories were real nail-biters.

Who do you like to fool? How is this like Hitchcock's fooling the audience? How is it different?

# TENSION AND FEAR WITH A LITTLE BIT OF HUMOR

A popular movie from 1975 was about a shark that attacked people. The special effects were simple compared to what we're used to these days. Still, it was a very scary movie. Its music set a suspenseful mood. It let the audience know when the shark was near, but they couldn't warn the characters, of course. The tension was almost too much. It's surprising to realize that the shark itself is first seen only late into the movie.

The makers of this movie played on people's fear of the unknown. There was a constant feeling that something awful was about to take place, but the people didn't know when.

Yet this movie, like many good mystery movies, has some humor. At a really scary moment, a character makes a joke or does something funny. The audience relaxes . . . and then wham! The unexpected happens.

In some movies, the bad guys are easy to spot. They may be invisible beings with a mean streak, apes about to take over Earth, or spacelings that spit poisonous goo and have metal fingernails. The mystery is there. The scare is there. Viewers know those characters are up to no good.

But suppose things seem peaceful, happy, and sunny. Audiences ready for action may think they've wandered into the wrong multiplex. Gotcha! Everyday events are scenes for many chilling suspense movies. The most ordinary people may turn out to be the scariest. Those chirping little birdies may turn out to be deadly. Daylight may hide just as many secrets as darkness does.

Why do people watch suspense movies? There are many reasons. But the most simple one may be this: We enjoy being scared—as long as we know it's just for fun and just a movie. ◉

Why would watching suspense movies be fun?

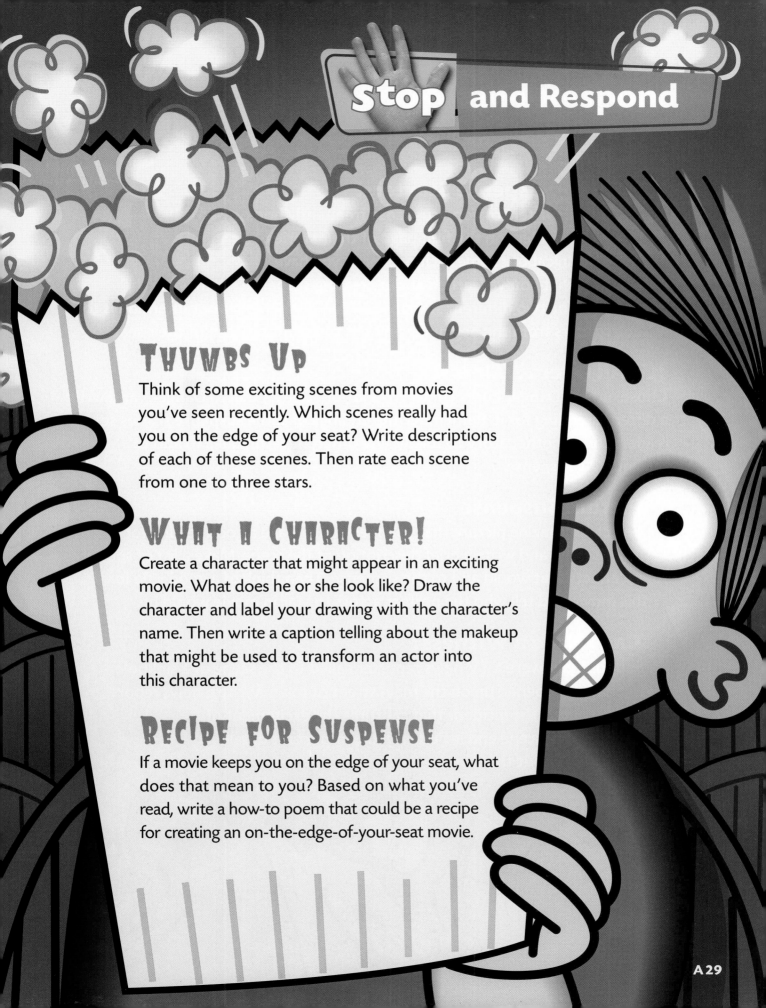

## THUMBS UP

Think of some exciting scenes from movies you've seen recently. Which scenes really had you on the edge of your seat? Write descriptions of each of these scenes. Then rate each scene from one to three stars.

## WHAT A CHARACTER!

Create a character that might appear in an exciting movie. What does he or she look like? Draw the character and label your drawing with the character's name. Then write a caption telling about the makeup that might be used to transform an actor into this character.

## RECIPE FOR SUSPENSE

If a movie keeps you on the edge of your seat, what does that mean to you? Based on what you've read, write a how-to poem that could be a recipe for creating an on-the-edge-of-your-seat movie.

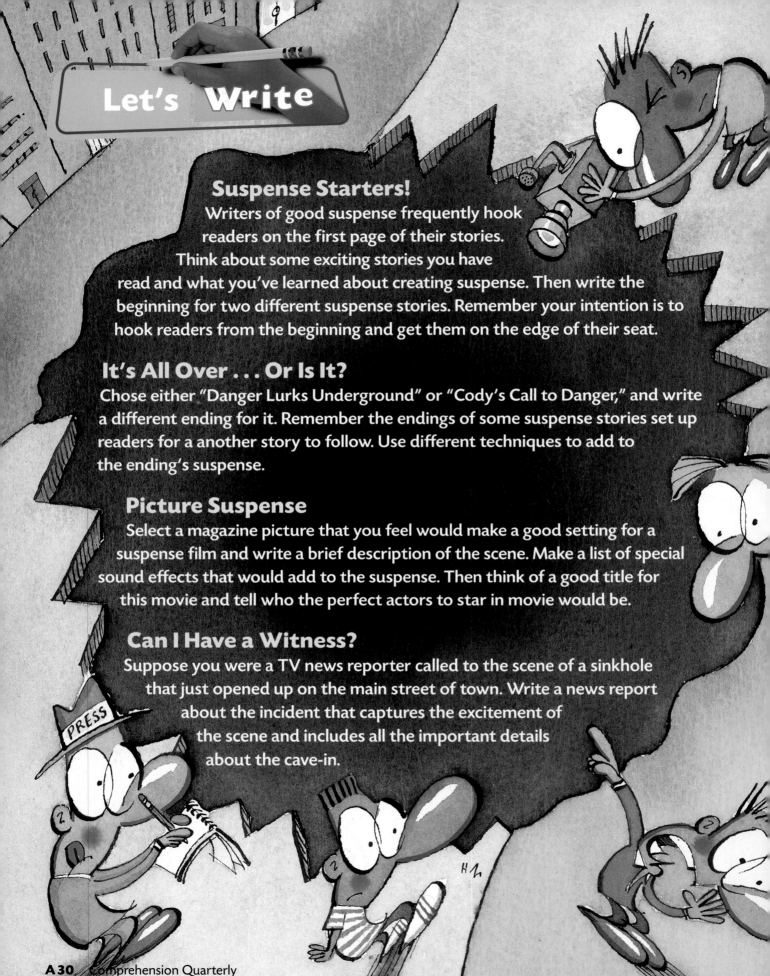

# Let's Write

## Suspense Starters!

Writers of good suspense frequently hook readers on the first page of their stories. Think about some exciting stories you have read and what you've learned about creating suspense. Then write the beginning for two different suspense stories. Remember your intention is to hook readers from the beginning and get them on the edge of their seat.

## It's All Over . . . Or Is It?

Chose either "Danger Lurks Underground" or "Cody's Call to Danger," and write a different ending for it. Remember the endings of some suspense stories set up readers for a another story to follow. Use different techniques to add to the ending's suspense.

## Picture Suspense

Select a magazine picture that you feel would make a good setting for a suspense film and write a brief description of the scene. Make a list of special sound effects that would add to the suspense. Then think of a good title for this movie and tell who the perfect actors to star in movie would be.

## Can I Have a Witness?

Suppose you were a TV news reporter called to the scene of a sinkhole that just opened up on the main street of town. Write a news report about the incident that captures the excitement of the scene and includes all the important details about the cave-in.

## More Books

Downs, Sandra. *When the Earth Moves.* Twenty-First Century Books, 2000.

Kehret, Peg. *Earthquake Terror.* Puffin, 1998.

Naylor, Phyllis Reynolds. *The Fear Place.* Atheneum, 1994.

Owen, Oliver S. *Cub to Grizzly Bear.* Abdo & Daughters, 1996.

Scott, Elaine. *Movie Magic: Behind the Scenes With Special Effects.* William Morrow & Co., 1995.

Stone, Lynn M. *Grizzlies.* Carolrhoda, 1993.

## On the Web

**Coal Mine Fires**
http://www.offroaders.com/album/
    centralia/centralia.htm
http://www.twilightheadquarters.com/
    snailtrailia.html

**Sinkholes**
http://ga.usgs.gov/edu/
    earthgwsinkholes.html

**Bear Dogs**
http://www.beardogs.org

**Special Effects**
http://www.pbs.org/wgbh/nova/
    specialfx2

## Across the Curriculum

### Art
With some classmates who have read the same exciting story you have, work together to illustrate the story. Your goal as illustrators is to make the drawings as exciting to look at as the story was to read.

### Science
Make a chart that compares what you have learned about Karelian Bear Dogs with the characteristics of another breed of dogs. Include comparisons and contrasts in physical features, behaviors, and countries of origin.

# On the Edge of a SEAT!

Your teacher says, "Take a seat." Which seat would you choose? How would you sit in it?

a student's desk?

a presidents chair?

or King Tut's throne?

COMPREHENSION QUARTERLY

# CQ⁴

**ISSUE B:** Monitoring

Journey Through Time

# Journey Through Time

## THINK ABOUT: Monitoring

**B4**

NONFICTION
### Through the Old West with Remington and Russell

These two "cowboy artists" have helped us picture the Old West—in more ways than one!

**B10**

FICTION
### An Adventure in Time

A field trip turns into something more than two curious kids expected.

**B18**

FICTION
### An Adventure in Time II

Another adventure? What's in store for Miguel and Lucinda this time?

**B24**

NONFICTION
### Life in the Past 100 Years

What was life like 100 years ago? More changes than you might believe!

## In this issue:

## MONITORING

# That's a Change!

"I don't want to do this report," complained Joe. "I don't care if sharks have been around forever. They're creepy! Who wants to read about them?"

"I do!" said his friend, Tony. "I think they're neat. Come on, Joe, take a look at this book. There's a whole chapter about sharks."

Joe sighed and took the book. At first, he just flipped pages, looking at the photographs. They only made him more sure that sharks were scary creatures.

Then finally, Joe started to read. Soon his head was filled with amazing facts about sharks. He started to write notes about the things he found especially interesting.

Joe finished the chapter and closed the book. "You were right," he told Tony. "Sharks are cool. Look what I found out so far." He handed the note cards to his friend.

Shark history
- Around for millions of years
- Haven't changed much since prehistoric times

How sharks help humans
- Help keep the ocean clean
- Used as food
- Used in research

"I can't wait to learn more," Joe continued. "Can I look at your book now?"

Careful readers **monitor** their reading and often find themselves changing their minds as they read. That's what Joe did. His first opinion of sharks was that they were scary and creepy. But his reading gave Joe new information. That information caused Joe to change his mind about sharks. And as he reads more, Joe will probably continue to change his mind and his thinking.

by Andrea Rains

# THROUGH THE OLD WEST
## with Remington and Russell

**L**isten carefully. Can you hear the hoofbeat of horses and the laughter of cowboys? They're coming through the rye. Try to imagine cowboys of the Old West—hot, dirty, and tired after long weeks, maybe even months, of cattle drives out on the wide, open range.

Once the cowboys spot a town, no trail boss can hold them back. They spur their horses into a wild gallop through the prairie grass, or rye, whooping and hollering.

It's easy to imagine such a scene with the help of frontier artist Frederic Remington. It's exactly the scene Remington created in his famous bronze sculpture, *Coming Through the Rye* (above).

**N**ow look closely at the work of another artist—Charles Russell. You can almost imagine yourself as part of the scene in his painting, *The Buffalo Hunt* (above). The thick, dry heat surrounds you as you pursue the small herd along the Sun River. You can smell the fresh earth kicked up from the buffalo, horses, and the Native Americans of the Great Plains.

Can you feel the spirit of the wild frontier when you look at these works of art?

Frederic Remington and Charles Russell were two artists who had a passion for the West. Their talent for painting, sculpting, and writing about the people and places of a time gone by has helped to document our heritage.

> What do you think Remington and Russell were like?

# WHO WAS FREDERIC REMINGTON?

Frederic Remington was born in New York in 1861—the same year the Civil War began. Remington's father had been in the military and hoped that his son would follow in his footsteps. But young Remington had different ideas. He had always loved horses and the rugged beauty of the western frontier, and when he was old enough, Remington's resistance to staying in the East led him out west to the land of his dreams.

During his years in the West, Remington worked as a cowboy and a farmer, and as a "hand," or helper, on a wagon train. But no matter where he went and what work he did, Remington took his paints with him. He realized that the Old West, as he knew it, was slowly vanishing. So as he traveled, Remington wrote about, drew, and painted everything he saw, heard, and felt.

In 1889, Remington won an international award for his painting. Other awards soon followed. Easterners were delighted with his tightly drawn, color "stories." After all, photographs from the newly invented camera were only in black and white. Remington's paintings, however, captured western beauty in all its splendid color.

Modern journals and magazines of the time published many of Remington's illustrations. In fact, his magazine illustrations were so popular that art buyers preferred to buy copies of those pieces instead of the original paintings.

But like memories of the West, paints fade. Remington knew this and was anxious to create a piece of art that would never vanish. In 1895, he sculpted *Bronco Buster,* his first sculpture in bronze. Art critics in Remington's time were amazed at the detail and perfection of his sculpture. Remington had found a new medium that promised to be more permanent than the scenes they preserved. From that point on, he continued to sculpt as well as paint.

*Cowboy on a Horse,* Frederic Remington, 1881–1909

# WHO WAS CHARLES RUSSELL?

Charles Russell was born in St. Louis, Missouri, in 1864. His parents wanted him to run the family business when he grew up, but like Frederic Remington before him, young Charlie Russell wanted to go west. When he was sixteen, Russell crossed the Mississippi River into the vast area of untamed land known as the American West. When he set out on his own, young Russell had no plans to be an artist. He worked first as a sheep farmer, then as a cowboy; but like Remington, he sketched and drew what he saw wherever he went. A newspaper reporter called him "the cowboy artist," and the name stuck with Russell for the rest of his life.

Charles Russell had great respect for the land and the customs of the Native American way of life. In fact, Russell considered the "Indian" to be the "true American." Sadly conscious that the Native American way of life was gradually disappearing, Russell was determined to preserve it on canvas before it was lost forever. His most brilliant and vibrant colors were used when he painted scenes from Native American life.

By his early twenties, Russell was recognized as one of the greatest western artists of his time. However, he still preferred to make a living as a cowboy and painted mainly as a hobby between his spring and fall trail drives. Resistant to changes in his routine, Russell continued to do most of his painting in his first art studio—the back room of an old saloon.

In 1903, Russell created his first sculpture in bronze. The sculpture, *Smoking Up,* shows a horse rearing up on its hind legs with a cowboy shooting his six-gun into the air. The sculpture was so popular that the president of the United States, Theodore Roosevelt, asked for one for the White House.

# THE WILD WEST IS SLOWLY TAMED

In the years after Remington and Russell moved west, many other Americans followed. For the American West, it was the beginning of the end. What had once been miles of prairie teeming with buffalo was soon becoming filled with pioneer families. And the "Wild West," as it had once been known, was becoming a little more tame with each covered wagon that rumbled across the prairie trails.

Yet more than a hundred years later, through the art of Frederic Remington and Charles Russell, we are still able to get a glimpse of that vast, untamed land. Through their writings, drawings, paintings, and sculptures, Remington and Russell left us a vivid picture of the West and the people who were once part of it. As Charles Russell himself said:

How differently do you see Remington and Russell now? What information in the text or photographs caused you to change your mind?

*Here's hoping your trail is a long one,*
*Plain and easy to ride.*
*May your dry camps be few*
*And health ride with you*
*To the pass on the Big Divide.* ○

*Cavalrymen in Battle,* Frederic Remington, 1890

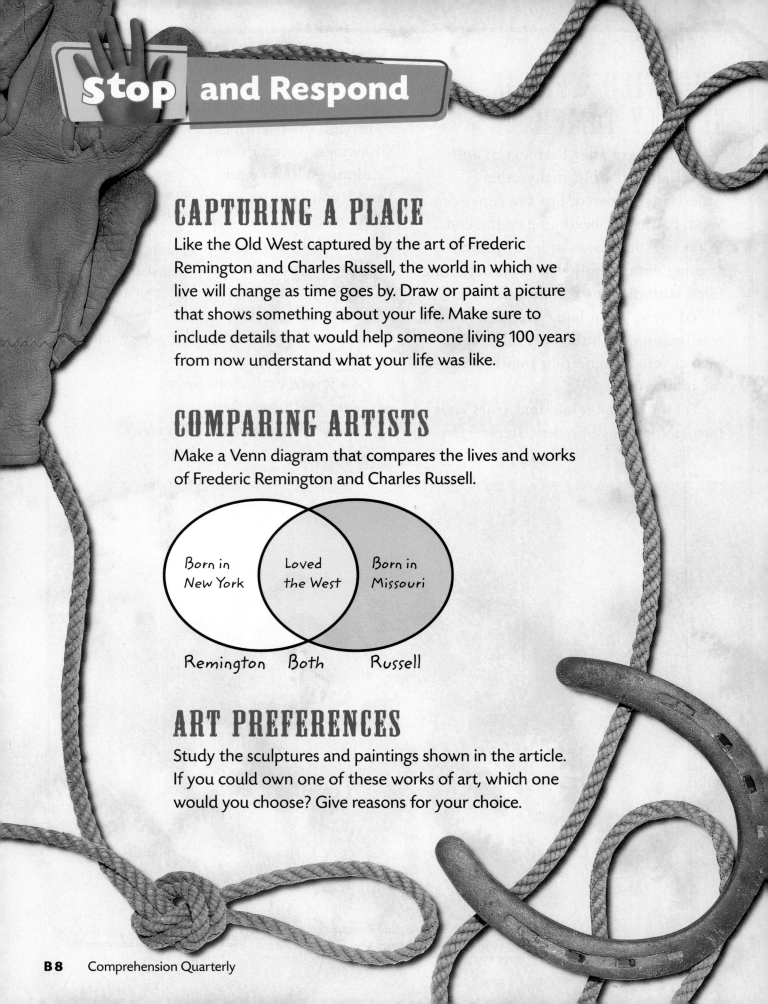

# Stop and Respond

## CAPTURING A PLACE

Like the Old West captured by the art of Frederic Remington and Charles Russell, the world in which we live will change as time goes by. Draw or paint a picture that shows something about your life. Make sure to include details that would help someone living 100 years from now understand what your life was like.

## COMPARING ARTISTS

Make a Venn diagram that compares the lives and works of Frederic Remington and Charles Russell.

Born in New York

Loved the West

Born in Missouri

Remington     Both     Russell

## ART PREFERENCES

Study the sculptures and paintings shown in the article. If you could own one of these works of art, which one would you choose? Give reasons for your choice.

# Moments in Time

Nothing captures a moment in time like a photograph. Thanks to Solomon Butcher, who traveled around the West photographing families, we can see into the lives of some of America's pioneers. What do these photos tell you about the way they lived?

How would you like to have horses on the roof and a built-in swing? What would it be like to live partly underground?

Look at the things piled up outside this house. How do you think each object might have been used?

Dugout on the South Loup River, Custer County, Nebraska, 1892. Nebraska State Historical Society

The Shores family, Westerville, Custer County, Nebraska, 1887. Nebraska State Historical Society

## Imagine That!

Choose one of the people pictured in these photographs and imagine that you are that person. From his or her point of view, write about your day during pioneer times.

# An Adventure in Time

## by Cynthia Mercati

"How's school?" Dad asked from behind his morning newspaper.

"Boring!" I answered. "My whole life is boring. I wish I'd lived a long time ago. You know, like in pioneer times."

Mom gave me a curious smile. "Why is that?"

"Because that's when life was really exciting," I said. "People had *real* adventures back then."

"What do you mean?" asked Dad. He pointed to an ad in the paper. "*EXCITING SALE TODAY AT BONTON'S DEPARTMENT STORE.*" He grinned. "See? There's excitement in Springdale."

As usual, Mom laughed at Dad's silly joke, and I groaned. Then Dad left for work, and Mom went upstairs to get ready for her job. I packed up my backpack, just like every other day.

"See you later!" I called to Mom as I went out the door. Halfway down the block, I met up with Miguel.

"Hola, Miguel," I greeted him.

"What's happenin', Lucinda?" he answered back.

"We're going to the Springdale Historical Museum today, remember?"

Miguel nodded. "How could I forget? We're going for burgers at lunch!"

We boarded the bus to the museum as soon as we got to school. At the museum, the first exhibit was about the geography of the prairie. I rushed right past it, straight to the frontier display.

There were photographs of pioneers and a big cyclorama that wrapped all the way around the room.

I stopped short in front of a life-sized model of a covered wagon. What would it feel like to sit on that, I wondered?

I looked around. Miguel and I were the only ones left in the room. Our teacher, Mrs. Fisher, and the rest of the class had moved on to another room.

Quick as a wink—or maybe even more quickly—I ducked under the ropes that surrounded the wagon and pulled myself up. Heart pounding, I sat down on the wagon bench.

I lifted imaginary reins in both hands. "Giddyup!" I called to my imaginary oxen. I waved to Miguel. "Come on up!"

Miguel climbed up, too. Then I crawled off the bench into the back of the wagon.

"It's as dark as night in here," I told Miguel.

Just then, a woman stuck her head through the canvas opening, a faded sunbonnet on her head. "Quit lollygaggin', you two," she said. She motioned us down. "Your Pa and I are waitin' to go!"

"Uh—yes, ma'am," I muttered.

Miguel and I jumped out of the wagon. Then we stopped and stared. The museum had disappeared, and the wide-open prairie stretched out in front of us! There were real oxen hitched to the wagon, yoked together in two teams of two. And I was no longer dressed in a T-shirt, jeans, and sneakers—instead I wore a long calico dress with an apron over it! My feet were bare and a bonnet was tied under my chin.

Miguel was wearing pants and a calico shirt that looked homemade and a straw hat. He was barefoot, too!

"We must have crossed through some kind of time portal," I whispered to Miguel.

"We've got to find a way to cross back to the present!" Miguel said. "I don't want to miss lunch."

"Stop thinking about your stomach!" I said. I was glad to be in the past—I couldn't wait for an adventure!

Pa patted one of the oxen. "I hope you critters remember you've got to make ten miles today!"

I rolled my eyes. Past or present, fathers said the silliest things.

Was the term *time portal* unfamiliar to you? How did you figure out its meaning? What clues does the text provide?

"Get yourself to the back of the wagon, daughter," Ma said, shooing me away. "You've got to look after the cow. You're in charge of her all the way to Springdale!"

"Springdale!" Miguel and I echoed.

"Your aunt and uncle are out there already, remember?" Ma said. "They wrote us it was a mighty fine place to build a homestead."

What do you think it would be like to live in pioneer times? Be prepared to change your thinking as you read on!

Miguel and I were on our way to settle in our own city! Maybe we'd even meet our own great-grandparents!

Pa climbed up to the wagon bench. He flapped the reins over the oxen's backs. Real reins! "Haw!" he shouted.

The animals strained forward. The wagon creaked and groaned. We were on our way!

Ma walked on one side of the oxen, with Miguel on the other side. The cow and I walked behind the wagon.

It wasn't hard to keep an eye on the cow, since she was tied to the back of the wagon with a rope. It wasn't hard walking either, but it sure was tiring. After a while, my feet started to blister.

"Hey, Ma," I shouted out. "When do I get to ride?"

Ma hooted with laughter. "Don't make jokes, daughter. You know we have to walk!"

I made a face. Maybe this going back in time thing wasn't going to be such a great idea after all.

The oxen kicked up a lot of dust. I felt like I was swallowing most of it. My teeth and tongue were coated with grit. And while the cow had a tail to swish away the flies and mosquitoes that swarmed around us, I was kept busy swatting and slapping them off me.

"These bugs are driving me crazy," I complained. In answer, Ma took a handful of something from a bucket tied to the wagon and smeared it all over my face.

I spit and sputtered. "What is this?" I demanded.

"Bacon fat, silly," she said. "Best thing for bites."

Miguel wrinkled up his nose as he caught a whiff. "You're gonna need a serious bath, my friend," he whispered.

When we stopped for the "nooning," as Pa called it, I thought I'd just crawl under the wagon and take a little nap. But Pa had other ideas. Miguel had to go down to the creek to fetch water, and I was told to gather up buffalo chips. Yuck!

"We need 'em to make the fire," said Ma. "There are no trees around here," she said.

Holding the chips by two fingers, I dropped them into my apron. At least they weren't squishy. But I sure didn't want to eat anything cooked on them! However, Miguel dug into his beans and bacon like they were a burger and fries.

After lunch, we started up again. I started picking wildflowers and knotting their stems together. Soon I had a whole wreath of flowers. Smiling, I slipped it around my neck, breathing in its fragrance.

I gazed around at the rolling hills. There was no doubt about it—the past was pretty. But I was already starting to miss hot showers and air-conditioning. And pizza!

*How did you figure out the meaning of the word nooning?*

Besides, I'd been in the past almost a whole day and I hadn't had one adventure yet.

But that was about to change. A river stood right in our path.

Pa looked for a good place to cross. Then he cut two long poles from the cottonwood trees growing by the water's edge. He handed one to me and one to Ma. "You two will have to pole the wagon across like a raft," he said. "Then the boy and I will swim the oxen across."

Ma took her place at the front of the wagon. She told me to stand at the back. Pa and Miguel pushed us into the water.

Ma stuck her pole into the water. I gritted my teeth and did the same. I was conscious of the butterflies in my stomach.

When we reached the middle of the river, the rapids under the surface suddenly gripped the wagon and turned it around. We tipped from side to side, water splashing up over the sides.

*This is it, Lucinda,* I told myself. *You're having your adventure! I just hope you survive it!*

I didn't feel excited—just scared.

The wagon dipped and swayed. I lost my balance and fell to my knees. I pushed up to my feet again and stuck my pole back into the water.

And then . . . we were on the other side!

"Good work, daughter," Ma said. I glowed with pride at her words.

Pa and Miguel unyoked the oxen and plunged them into the river. Cautiously, Miguel put one hand against one ox's side and used his other hand to swim.

When Miguel got to the other side, we gave each other a high-five. "We did it!"

*Maybe that was the point of having adventures,* I thought, *learning something*

Have you changed your mind about what it would be like to live in pioneer times? What information in the text caused you to feel this way?

*about yourself. Learning that when the chips were down—and I don't mean buffalo chips—you could do something difficult!*

I guess I'd learned something about the past today. It wasn't all that different from the present! Oh, sure, it was harder in some ways. But walking behind a wagon could be just as boring as sitting in a classroom.

"Fetch us some blankets, children," Ma said.

I swung myself into the back of the wagon. Miguel climbed in behind me.

It was pitch dark again. As we pushed aside the canvas opening to come back out, we found ourselves back in the museum.

We were back in our own time again!

Miguel shook his head as if trying to clear it. "Wow," he breathed.

"Wow is right," I agreed. "That was totally weird—but cool!"

We heard Mrs. Fisher's voice calling from the hall, "Back on the bus, everyone!"

"Burgers!" Miguel called out. In a flash, he climbed down from the wagon and disappeared out the door. I still sat on the wagon, trying to figure things out.

We'd been in the past almost the whole day, but not much time had passed in the present. How could that be?

Then the answer hit me. I must have dreamed the whole thing! *But it seemed so real,* I thought to myself.

"Come on, Lucinda," Mrs. Fisher called out, appearing at the door again.

"Sorry," I said and scrambled down. As I hurried by Mrs. Fisher, she stopped me. She lifted up the wilted wildflower garland that hung around my neck.

"Where did you get this?" she asked, puzzled.

My hand flew to my neck to touch the necklace. My mouth dropped open and my stomach lurched. *Now, where had I gotten it?* ◯

# Stop and Respond

### Whoa! What's Going On?

What were you thinking as you read this article? Name one section that made you change your mind about what was going on. Then think about how the story ended. Did you change your ideas about what actually happened to Lucinda and Miguel? Talk to a classmate or write your ideas in your journal.

### Best and Worst

Imagine that you are suddenly taken back to pioneer times. What do you think would be the best thing about living then? What would be the worst? Write a paragraph that explains your thoughts.

### Make a Cyclorama

A cyclorama is a round mural. Make a miniature cyclorama that shows what life was like in pioneer times or in another time that interests you. Tape or staple four sheets of drawing paper end-to-end to make one strip. Draw scenes on the long strip. Then tape the two ends together so your drawings are facing out.

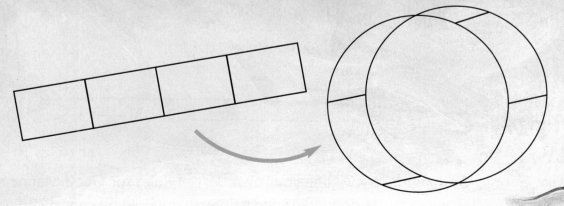

George Washington's **MANNERS**

Things change over time—even what we think of as good manners! In George Washington's day, young people were expected to learn many rules for good behavior. In fact, as a young boy, Washington filled ten pages of a notebook with rules for good manners. He called it "Rules for Civility and Decent Behavior in Company and Conversation." Here are some of his rules:

In the presence of others, do not sing with a humming noise, nor drum with your fingers or feet.

If you cough, sneeze, sigh, or yawn, do it not loudly but privately … put your handkerchief over your face and turn aside.

Sleep not when others speak, sit not when others stand, speak not when you should hold your peace, walk not when others stop.

Turn not your back to others, especially in speaking …

Show not yourself glad at the misfortune of another even though he may be your enemy.

Washington, George. "Rules of Civility and Decent Behavior in Company and Conversation." Circa 1747. *The George Washington Papers.*

AcHoo?

Very uncouth!

Tsk, tsk!

z

## Try It Yourself!

Like George Washington, try writing your own "List of Rules for Good Manners and Proper Behavior." Write down ten suggestions that would be considered good manners today. How do your rules compare with George Washington's list?

## MONITORING
# Stopping to Think

Maria was doing some research about life in medieval times. She found an interesting article about food and how it was served. As she was reading the article, Maria was confused. She had to stop, reread more slowly, and use other monitoring strategies to help her understand the text.

A medieval feast was a grand occasion. However, some things about the meal weren't the same for everyone.

The lord's table was set up on a small dais. The other tables, called trestle tables, were on a lower level. This let the lord look down on everyone else.

Those who sat at the lord's table were the only ones who had chairs. Everyone else sat on rough benches.

Tables were set with cups, spoons, and trenchers. Trenchers were slabs of bread which were used as plates. On the lord's table, serving platters were made of silver. On the other tables, they were made of wood.

> Hmmm. What is a **dais?** By reading the next sentence, I can figure out that it must be some kind of platform. But I need to check the dictionary to see how to pronounce the word.

> What is a **trencher?** I'd better read on to see if it tells me.

> I see—this article compares and contrasts the lord's table with the other tables.

Maria **monitors** her own comprehension by stopping to ask herself questions as she reads. She adjusts her reading pace and answers her questions by reading on, using the context, and reviewing what she has read. All of these strategies help Maria make sense of what she reads.

# An Adventure in TIME II

## by Cynthia Mercati

I plopped the breakfast dishes in the sink. "We need a dishwasher," I said.

"We *have* a dishwasher, Lucinda," said Dad, grinning. "You!"

"I mean it," I said. "This family lives in the past! We need to move into the future!"

As Mom packed her coffee thermos, she said, "I thought you were more interested in the past."

I *had* been more interested in the past until I'd actually *gone* there. But I didn't say that to Mom. All I said was, "People had to work too hard in the past. In the future, we'll have machines to do all our work for us."

I slung my backpack over one shoulder and started out the door. I met up with Miguel halfway down the block.

I couldn't wait to get to school. Our class was going to the museum to see another exhibit today. This one was "Springdale in the Future." I couldn't wait!

Once we got to school, we all piled onto a bus and headed for the museum. There were lots of displays, but the one that interested me the most was a telephone booth in one corner. It was tall and narrow and

shiny and had a cone on the top. It certainly didn't look like anything I'd ever seen before. I couldn't resist touching it. When I did, the door swung open.

*That's funny,* I thought. *But since the door was already open . . .*

I looked around. No one was watching. Hesitantly, I stepped into the booth.

"Miguel," I whispered, motioning him toward the phone booth. As soon as he squeezed in, the door swung shut.

The inside of the booth was as shiny as the outside. I picked up a receiver that looked like a crescent moon. "Hello? Is anybody there?"

To my amazement, a pleasant voice answered. "Good morning. May I help you?"

"How could someone be on the other end?" I asked Miguel.

"Maybe it's a recording," he suggested.

I spoke into the receiver again. "Could you please connect me with the future?"

"The future is closer than you think," the same voice answered. "Just step outside."

We stepped out of the booth to find ourselves on a rapidly moving sidewalk.

All the people around us were dressed in silvery, silky jumpsuits. Miguel and I looked down at our own clothes. We were wearing the same jumpsuits!

We looked around. Shiny buildings towered over us, and sleek trains rushed by on tracks suspended in the air. Swift cars glided down the street, like silent, silver bugs. Inside, the occupants were eating, reading—even sleeping. But no one was driving!

Just then we saw a sign outside one of the buildings. Miguel and I read the words.

"Springdale City Hall"

We had crossed through a time portal again. Only this time, we'd landed right in the middle of our city's future!

"How could Springdale be this big?" asked Miguel. "Look!" He pointed to one of the buildings that loomed ahead. On it was a sign that said SPRINGDALE ELEMENTARY SCHOOL.

"Let's check it out," I said, and pushed the "stop" button on the handrail. The moving sidewalk slowed, and we hopped off and ran toward the school.

A spacious glass dome was connected to the school by a long tunnel with lots of windows. We walked around the perimeter of the dome—we couldn't believe it was so huge! As we neared the entrance, a computer demanded, "Please press your right hand to the screen."

What do you predict will happen to Miguel and Lucinda in the future? Why do you think this?

As we did, the computer said, "Thank you, Miguel and Lucinda. Your handprints have been scanned and recorded. Feel free to move around the dome and school. And have a nice day!"

"Thanks," Miguel answered cautiously.

Inside the dome was a large playground area. Trees and flowering bushes grew everywhere, while brightly colored birds flitted around. The guardian eyes of the computers constantly scanned the playground, watching over the children.

Skateboarders and skaters shot by us. But the kids were only passengers—we could see that their boards and blades were also controlled by the computer.

Miguel and I headed for a giant slide. A chair lift, like the ones at a ski resort,

How have you figured out some of the challenging vocabulary in this story? How do you adjust your reading pace when you come to difficult words?

carried us to the top. Miguel sat down at the top of the slide and gave me a thumbs-up sign. Then with a swooshing sound, he took off.

When it was my turn, I held on to the slide's guardrails with both hands. "One, two, three," I muttered under my breath. I felt like an Olympic bobsledder. I pushed off, eyes squeezed shut. I couldn't believe the feeling. It was like riding on a roller coaster! When I got to the bottom, Miguel and I high-fived each other.

We tried out the swings next. I noticed that we wouldn't have to use our legs on these swings—they were powered by a computer.

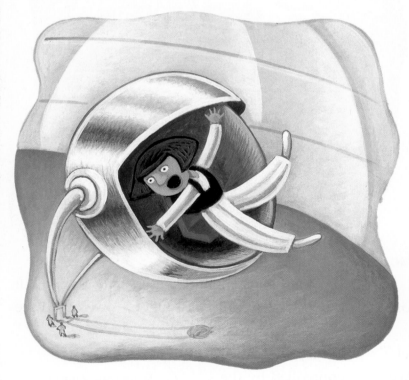

I strapped myself into one of the pods, and it took off immediately. The swing arced higher and higher and higher until I was so high, I could almost touch the top of the dome. Then all at once, the pod plunged

down, then back up again, and over in a loop-de-loop. I screamed as I felt my stomach lurch. It was great!

A buzzer buzzed then, and all the children lined up. Miguel and I followed them through the tunnel and into the school. Miguel asked a computer for directions to the gym.

"Twelfth floor," the computer replied. "Take the elevator to your right."

Were any of your predictions about the future correct? How have you changed your mind as you read this story?

The elevator opened directly into the gym. Two lines of kids about our age and dressed in silvery uniforms were shaking hands with one another.

"The game must have just ended," Miguel said. He read the scoreboard aloud, his voice rising in disbelief. "Springdale, 322. Visitors, 221! Could that be right?"

A boy and a girl on the Springdale team approached us. "Can we help you?" the girl asked.

"You sure can," Miguel said. "How did you score so many points?"

The boy laughed. "Maybe it's because our team just got brand new flyers—they really made a difference!"

"What are flyers?" I asked.

"Basketball shoes," the girl said. She pointed down at her silver-soled high-top shoes. Small lights blinked and beeped all along the outside of each shoe.

"I thought every team wore flyers now," the boy said. He peered at us curiously. "Where are you from?" he asked.

I quickly asked, "Could you show us how your new flyers work?"

"Sure," the girl said. She started running down the court. Then she picked up speed—and flew into the air! When she was level with the basket, the boy threw her the ball. Then the girl dropped it in. It was unbelievable!

The two ran back to us. "My name is Sunny," the boy said. He pointed to his friend. "This is Skye. Want to play a pickup game? You can try out the flyers."

"Two on two, first team to get to ten wins," Skye said.

"A game would be great," I said, "but why don't we play without flyers?"

"We've never done that before," Sunny said, surprised. "But it might be fun."

Skye's face broke into a wide grin. "Let's give it a try!"

The four of us took off our shoes and the game began.

Miguel and I weren't on a real team back home—we just shot baskets with kids from our neighborhood in each other's driveways. We certainly didn't feel too confident playing against these two. But we did have one advantage—we were used to scrambling for every point. We had to. We didn't have anything to depend on but ourselves. Soon the score was 8 to 8.

Sunny went in for a layup and missed. Miguel grabbed the rebound. He tossed the ball to me. I dodged around Skye and charged the basket. I jumped for all I was worth.

My jump wasn't anything compared to the jump I could have made in flying shoes. But I did it all on my own.

I sank the shot. We won!

"That was a great workout!" Skye said, panting.

"Hey, where can we get a good burger and fries?" Miguel asked. "I'm starving!"

"What else is new?" I muttered.

"They make great kelp burgers at the restaurant down the street," Sunny said. "And their seaweed fries are the best."

"Kelp!" Miguel squeaked like someone in pain. "Seaweed! You've gotta be kidding! I want real meat—and real potatoes!"

"Well, it was great meeting you guys," Sunny said, looking at Miguel strangely. "We've got to hit the showers. Maybe we'll see you later at the 'Springdale in the Past' exhibit on the 14th floor." And they headed off the court, holding their flyers by the laces.

Miguel was mumbling to himself. "Kelp? Seaweed? Yuck!"

I snapped my fingers in his face. "Earth to Miguel! Get your mind off food. Let's take a look at that exhibit."

We put on our shoes and took the elevator to the exhibit. Inside, we found all kinds of things we had at home. The kids around us were amazed by things they thought were ancient!

That's when Miguel noticed the telephone booth in the corner.

"Maybe that's our ticket out of here," I said.

"Yeah," said Miguel. "The future is definitely interesting—but I don't think I could take the food. Are you ready to go?"

I thought about Miguel's question. On one hand, the Springdale of tomorrow was dazzling. On the other hand, I was starting to miss the nice little city I called home. Bigger, I decided, wasn't necessarily better.

I missed doing things for myself, too. I thought people in the future probably had everything too easy. They didn't have to drive their own cars, or do the dishes, or any of the other chores I complained about. But they didn't know what it was like to score a winning basket all on their own, either. I decided I didn't want to lose that feeling.

"Yeah, I'm ready to leave, too," I said.

We stepped inside the phone booth and I picked up the receiver. "We'd like to get back to the present," I said.

"Just step outside," the familiar voice answered.

"Alright!" Miguel shouted. "I can almost smell lunch!"

We walked out of the booth—and back into the Springdale Historical Museum. I looked around. Yup, it was the same old building, same old everything. Outside the window, the same old cars were going by—and they were being driven by people!

"Well, we've gone back in time *and* ahead," Miguel said, scratching his head. "Compared to the future, life here is pretty slow. But compared to the past, it's pretty fast! And a lot more comfortable." He shook his head. "I'm not sure which I like better."

I was silent a moment, remembering everything I'd seen on our two amazing trips.

"*I* think they're both great," I said slowly but decisively, "but the important thing is to make the most out of where you are—and that's the present!" ●

Was the "future" what you expected it to be like? How have you changed your mind about living in the future after reading this story?

# READING FIX-UPS

List two or three words or sentences that you found difficult or confusing as you were reading the story. Then think about how you made sense of those words or sentences. Did you slow down? Did you read on to see if the rest of the text would help explain things? Did you ask another reader for help? Did you use a reference tool, like a dictionary? Compare with a classmate some of the fix-up strategies you used when you had difficulty with the text. Did you and your classmate use any of the same strategies?

# INVENT THE FUTURE

The future could bring anything from "smell-o-vision" to sneakers that let you fly! Think of a future invention that would make your life easier or more fun. Draw your invention and write a brief description of it.

# POETIC THOUGHTS

Create an acrostic poem about life in the future. First, write the word FUTURE down the side of a sheet of paper, with one letter under the other. Then write your poem, beginning each line with the letter shown at the beginning. Your poem can be rhymed or unrhymed.

F ood will cook without a stove.
U ltra-fast rocket ships will let us rove.
T
U
R
E

# Life in the

On December 17, 1903, in Kitty Hawk, North Carolina, something amazing happened. Orville and Wilbur Wright flew an airplane. It was the first time in history anyone had ever done that, and it changed the nature of travel forever. Just 66 years later, in 1969, man flew to the moon.

## Life in the United States in 1903

Much has changed between 1903 and the present. Not only had no one flown an airplane before 1903, but there were very few automobiles. Cars were a new invention, and few people could afford to own one. People traveled long distances by train and by steamship.

In 1903, the greatest change to everyday life was electricity. Businesses had electricity, but most homes did not. Over the next 30 years, electric lights gradually replaced gaslights in homes.

People baked their own bread, cakes, pies, and cookies, and stored their food in *iceboxes*. The icebox held a large block of ice in a bottom compartment that kept everything cold, but every few days, the iceman had to deliver a new block of ice.

Many homes had central heat from coal-burning furnaces. Heat rose through pipes into each room and out through radiators. Even with these improvements, it still took a long time to heat water, so most people had a bath only once a week. Not everyone had an indoor toilet. Those who didn't had to use an outhouse.

More and more households had a telephone. In 1903, people spoke into a mouthpiece to tell an operator what number they wanted. Many families used the same telephone line, called a *party line,* on which you had to wait your turn to make a call. The *wireless* was another new invention, which led to what we call today a radio.

What strategies did you use when you came to unfamiliar terms, such as *icebox* and *wireless*?

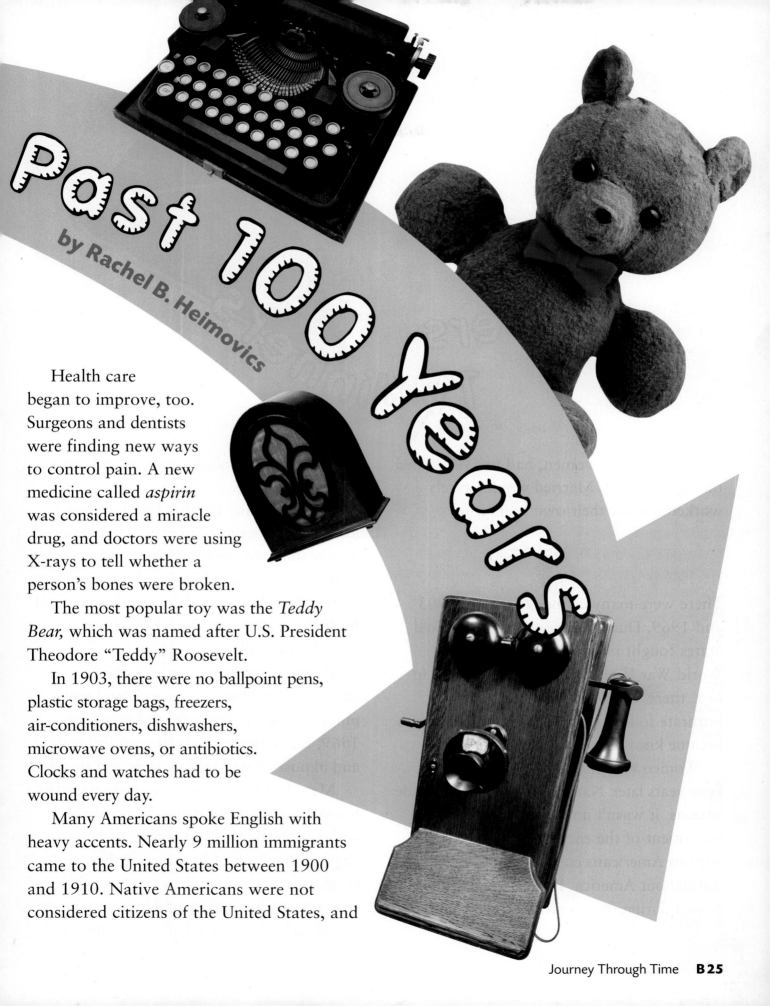

# Past 100 Years

by Rachel B. Heimovics

Health care began to improve, too. Surgeons and dentists were finding new ways to control pain. A new medicine called *aspirin* was considered a miracle drug, and doctors were using X-rays to tell whether a person's bones were broken.

The most popular toy was the *Teddy Bear,* which was named after U.S. President Theodore "Teddy" Roosevelt.

In 1903, there were no ballpoint pens, plastic storage bags, freezers, air-conditioners, dishwashers, microwave ovens, or antibiotics. Clocks and watches had to be wound every day.

Many Americans spoke English with heavy accents. Nearly 9 million immigrants came to the United States between 1900 and 1910. Native Americans were not considered citizens of the United States, and

Baby Boomers

TV dinners

they, along with women, had not yet gained the right to vote. Married women rarely worked outside their own homes.

## Life in the United States in 1969

There were many changes between 1903 and 1969. During these years, the United States fought in two world wars. After World War II, many babies were born. In fact, there was such a "boom" in the birthrate following the war that these babies became known as *baby boomers*.

Women won the right to vote in 1920. Four years later, Native Americans were made citizens. It wasn't until the Civil Rights movement of the early 1960s that many African Americans enjoyed equal rights throughout America. Federal laws were passed during these years that protected all

Americans in schools, businesses, and other public institutions.

In 1969, many families began to move away from cities into suburbs. They shopped in new shopping malls and large supermarkets instead of small neighborhood grocery stores. Food stores sold frozen dinners, and fresh fruits and vegetables were flown in from faraway places.

People went to movies, watched television, and listened to rock-and-roll music on radios, records, and tapes. By 1969, many homes were air-conditioned, and almost all had refrigerators and freezers.

Manufacturers were using new materials for many household items. Unbreakable, colorful plastic was one material that changed the look of furniture, dishes, and eyeglasses, and made them last longer. New wooden products and metal mixtures made tennis rackets and baseball bats lighter and stronger. And clothing made of nylon and polyester could be washed and packed without wrinkling.

Students typed school papers on electric typewriters, and some offices even had computers. These computers were large and stood on the floor, but they were a lot smaller than the computers from the 1950s, which were as large as a small house.

By 1969, children were being vaccinated against such diseases as polio. Surgeons were transplanting kidneys and hearts. Antibiotics and other new medicines helped fight diseases. Tiny scopes had been invented to allow doctors to look inside people's bodies for clues to their illnesses.

In 1969, most travel was done by airplane and automobile. Superhighways crisscrossed the nation. Jets took off regularly at airports throughout the nation, and new supersonic, high-speed airplanes could travel at more than 1,300 miles per hour.

But perhaps America's greatest achievements were in space exploration. Since the end of World War II, the United States and the Soviet Union had been pitted against each other in a bitter rivalry known as the Cold War. These two superpowers had raced against each another to build better weapons and space programs. When the Soviet Union was the first to send a man into space in 1961, the U.S. worked even

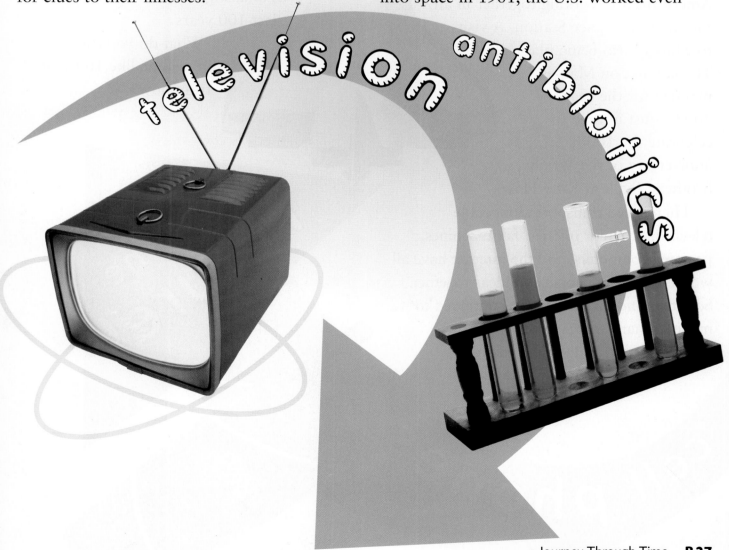

television  antibiotics

harder to outdo them. The U.S. set a goal to reach the moon by the end of the '60s, and on July 20, 1969—only 66 years after the Wright brothers made their famous flight at Kitty Hawk—Americans Neil Armstrong and Edwin Aldrin, who had traveled 186,000 miles through space, walked on the moon.

*How do you adjust the pace of your reading to understand an article like this one, which has so much information?*

## Life at the Beginning of the 21st Century

As we begin the 21st century, the Cold War is over, and Russians and Americans are working together in an International Space Station. A visit to Mars is also being planned. The landing on Mars is planned for the year 2003—just in time to celebrate the 100th anniversary of the Wright brothers' flight at Kitty Hawk.

High-speed transportation, cable television, cellular phones, fax machines, personal computers, and the Internet have all worked to bring people and ideas together. Scientists and inventors have continued to make so many things in our lives safer, stronger, faster, and less expensive.

But the new century holds many challenges yet to be met. Concerns about the environment, endangered animals, population growth, new health issues, and the threat of nuclear weapons are all problems that will need solutions in the coming century. As always, however, there will be people—including young people like you—who help solve these problems and others that arise. What does the future hold? We can only guess. The only thing that *is* certain is that the next 100 years will bring change as amazing as the last 100 years.

*After reading this article, how has your thinking changed about life in the past 100 years?*

What do *you* think life will be like 100 years from now? ⊙

Into the Future!

cell phones

# Stop and Respond

## Looking for Help

Think back to the article "Life in the Past 100 Years." The author writes about many inventions and advancements in the last century. List two or three that you don't know much about. Then write some ideas for learning more about these topics. For example, if you want to know about the Internet, you might ask an adult who works with computers. Or if you want to know about airplanes, you might look in an encyclopedia.

## What If?

Imagine how different life would be if people like the Wright brothers hadn't worked so hard to bring their ideas to life. Choose one invention from the list below. Write a paragraph that tells how your life might be different if this item hadn't been invented.

airplane   telephone   electric light
automobile   radio   television
Internet   microwave

## Problems and Solutions

Sometimes the solutions to old problems cause new problems that no one ever expected. Look at the example below. Then list two more examples.

**Problem:** Farmers need to grow more crops to feed more people.

**Solution:** Chemicals are used to kill insects that eat food crops.

**New Problem:** The chemicals pollute the soil and water.

Think about some of the problems that people have faced in the last 50 years and some of the solutions they have found for those problems. Were new problems created by any of the solutions?

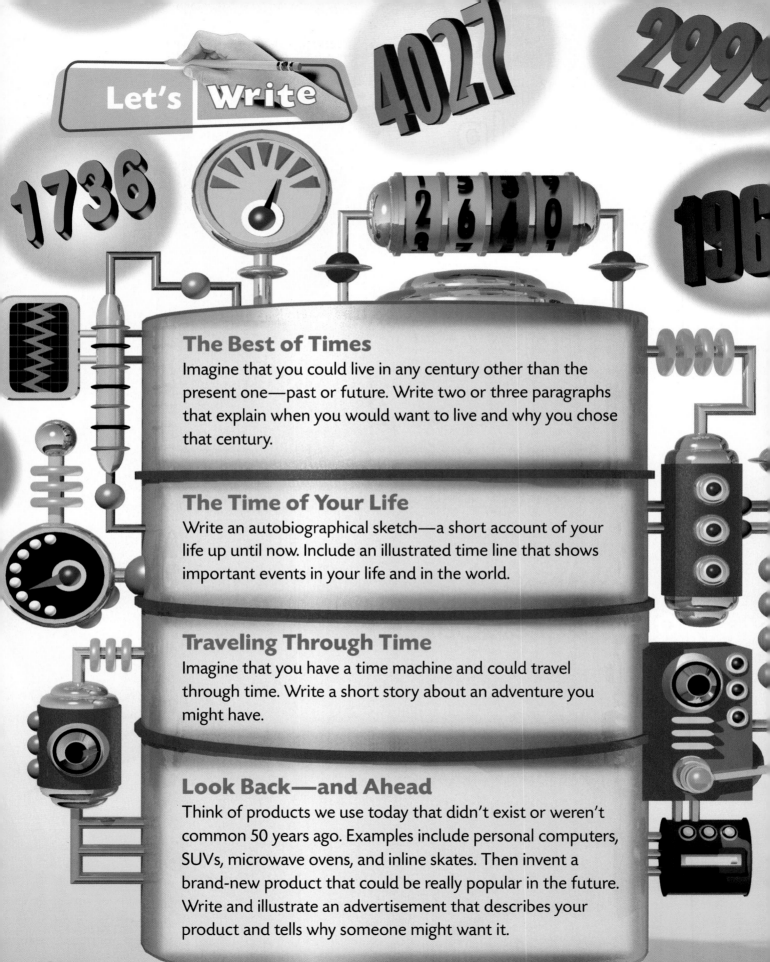

## Let's Write

### The Best of Times

Imagine that you could live in any century other than the present one—past or future. Write two or three paragraphs that explain when you would want to live and why you chose that century.

### The Time of Your Life

Write an autobiographical sketch—a short account of your life up until now. Include an illustrated time line that shows important events in your life and in the world.

### Traveling Through Time

Imagine that you have a time machine and could travel through time. Write a short story about an adventure you might have.

### Look Back—and Ahead

Think of products we use today that didn't exist or weren't common 50 years ago. Examples include personal computers, SUVs, microwave ovens, and inline skates. Then invent a brand-new product that could be really popular in the future. Write and illustrate an advertisement that describes your product and tells why someone might want it.

## More Books

Banks, Lynne Reid. *The Indian in the Cupboard*. Avon, 1995.

Bellairs, John. *The Ghost in the Mirror*. Penguin, 1994.

Jackson, Ellen. *Turn of the Century*. Charlesbridge, 1998.

L'Engle, Madeleine. *A Wrinkle in Time*. Scholastic, 1997.

Langton, Jane. *The Time Bike*. Harper Collins, 2000.

Van Steenwyk, Elizabeth. *Frederic Remington*. Watts, 1994.

## On the Web

**Charles Russell**
http://www.falconoutdoors.com/
cmrussell/index.cfm

**Frederic Remington Works**
http://www.canvascreations.com/
gallery/Remington.html

**Frederic Remington Sculptures**
http://www.intercom.net/biz/objdart/
galremi.html

## Across the Curriculum

### Social Studies

Gather materials for a personal, family, or classroom time capsule. Select objects that would show people 10, 50, or even 100 years from now what your life is like. You might include newspaper articles and advertisements, small toys, photographs, a tape recording or CD, and so on. Place all the objects in a waterproof container. On the outside of the container, write the date you filled the capsule and the date it should be opened.

### Language Arts

Interview an older neighbor or family member to find out about changes that have taken place during that person's lifetime. Before the interview, list questions you want to ask. Remember to thank your interview subject for his or her time.

# Timely Sayings

There are many sayings about time. But what do they mean? Read the "time-ly" sayings below and see if you know what they mean. If you need help, ask your teacher!

When someone says that **time flies,** what do they mean?

If you do something **in no time** at all, how do you do it?

If you take a **time out,** what are you doing?

If you **pass the time of day** with someone, what are you doing?

If something happens **time after time,** when does it happen?

If you are **killing time,** what are you doing?

## Try It Yourself!

With a partner, try to think of some more sayings that have to do with time. Try them out on your classmates to see if they know what the sayings mean!

10:34

COMPREHENSION QUARTERLY

# CQ

4

**ISSUE C:** Synthesizing

It's a Family Affair!

# It's a Family Affair!

## THINK ABOUT: Synthesizing

**NONFICTION**
### They Call Her Maria
Maria Martinez is famous for her black-on-black pottery. Find out how she became a legendary potter.

C11

C4

**FICTION**
### Reynaldo's Magic Stripes
Read about the special relationship Reynaldo has with his Aunt Meche and what he learns from her.

C19

**NONFICTION**
### A Walk in the Woods
Come along as we watch eagles and black bears in their natural habitats.

C25

**FICTION**
### The Wedding
Mom is getting remarried and she wants her son Mark to walk her down the aisle. What will he do?

## SYNTHESIZING

# A Recommendation

Readers **synthesize** every time they read. This means that they organize different parts of what they are reading in their minds in order to understand the whole text. Readers do the same thing when they recommend or criticize a book to a friend. They share just the parts of the book that tell about the important events or characters and that support their opinions as readers. They don't retell every detail of the whole story.

Read Sumi's synthesis of *Charlie and the Chocolate Factory* below.

**Sumi:** Hey, Dad, we just finished *Charlie and the Chocolate Factory,* by Roald Dahl.

**Mr. Shigato:** I don't think I remember that one. What is it about?

**Sumi:** It's a great book. The characters in the story are such brats, except for Charlie, the main character. But the rest of the kids have no manners. Anyway, Charlie was the lucky holder of the fifth golden ticket to tour Willy Wonka's chocolate factory.

**Mr. Shigato:** Now I'm starting to remember the story.

**Sumi:** The characters had funny names like Augustus Gloop and Veruca Salt. They acted like spoiled kids. Mr. Wonka didn't seem to like them much, probably because of their bad behavior.

**Mr. Shigato:** So what happened to the winners?

**Sumi:** Well, everyone got what they deserved. And Charlie ended up getting the factory!

**Mr. Shigato:** Guess it pays to behave!

When you discuss something you've read with a friend and you share the important parts, you're synthesizing. Share a synthesis of a book you've recently read with a friend.

# Reynaldo's Magic STRIPES

## by Katacha Díaz

**O**ne morning at dawn, when the sun was slowly making its way over the desert hills, Reynaldo put on his jacket and tiptoed out of the house.

He hurried down the road toward the town's *placita* where Aunt Meche lived.

"Cook-cook, cook-cook," called the roadrunner from atop the cholla cactus, where she sat in her nest with an early morning catch—a big fat lizard!

"Good morning, Mrs. Roadrunner," he said.

Reynaldo lived in the tiny mountain village of Río Chiquito in northern New Mexico. Reynaldo's father was a farmer. His mother was a teacher. And his

*Tía* Meche was a weaver, one of the best in the Río Grande valley.

*Tía* Meche lived across the road in an old *adobe* house that was also her weaving workshop.

"*Buenos días*, Reynaldo. I'm glad to see you," said *Tía* Meche.

"*Buenos días, Tía*," Reynaldo said. "What plants do we need today, *Tía*?" he asked.

"The recipe calls for prickly pear fruit and *chamisa*," she answered.

Reynaldo knew *Tía* Meche's recipes were the same ones his ancestors had used many, many years ago to make the natural dyes to color yarn. The ingredients were a guarded family secret. *Tía* Meche kept the old, tattered recipe book locked up in a wooden box on her desk.

Soon they came upon a giant prickly pear cactus covered with lots of ripe fruit.

"Don't forget your cactus-picking gloves," *Tía* Meche reminded him. "They'll keep those nasty little prickly spines from getting into your fingers!"

Reynaldo and *Tía* Meche picked the fruit and rubbed each piece in the sand to remove the spines. Soon the basket was full.

Reynaldo ran down the dirt path ahead of *Tía* Meche and headed toward the *arroyo*, or stream. Alongside the *arroyo* grew a *chamisa*, a wild green bush covered with bright yellow flowers in bloom. He quickly filled the basket with blossoms and twigs, and headed back up the path where he caught up with *Tía* Meche. They started back toward the village.

They crossed the road and headed toward the *placita* and *Doña* Tomasita's store. It was the only general store in the village. She sold a little bit of everything.

"*Buenos días, comadre*," said *Tía* Meche. "Any news about my special order?"

"*Sí, comadre*," *Doña* Tomasita replied. She reached under the counter, pulled out a brown paper bag, and handed it to *Tía* Meche.

"*Gracias, comadre*," said *Tía* Meche, smiling.

Back at his aunt's house, Reynaldo helped fill large pots with water and carried them outside. Meanwhile, *Tía* Meche built a small fire in the courtyard. Reynaldo carefully placed the pots on the grill over the flames.

"Are you ready to grind the bugs?" *Tía* Meche asked Reynaldo.

What one thing has caught your attention so far in this story? Why?

"Bugs!" he cried. "What kind of bugs?"

"*Cochineal*," she answered. *Tía* Meche reached inside the paper bag from *Doña* Tomasita's store and took a handful of the dead, silver, ash-gray insects. She put them on the family's old grinding stone for Reynaldo to grind.

"This is an ancient tradition," *Tía* Meche explained. "*Cochineal* bugs make the brightest red dye there is. You'll see."

Reynaldo grinded away. Soon all that was left was a fine powder.

When the water began to boil, Reynaldo took some of the *cochineal* powder, prickly pear fruit, and *chamisa* flowers and dropped them into each pot. Then *Tía* Meche added a handful of their secret family ingredient, and dropped the yarn into the pots. Several hours later, Reynaldo and *Tía* Meche carefully draped the now colorful yarn over the clothesline to dry in the hot desert sun.

The next morning, Reynaldo put on his jacket and ran over to *Tía* Meche's house. He found her weaving away in the workshop. Reynaldo watched *Tía* Meche's hands quickly glide the old wooden shuttle between the warp threads. It was like magic! Her body wobbled in a seesaw rhythm as she worked the foot pedals. Clickity-clack, clickity-clack went the old loom.

"What are you making, *Tía*?" Reynaldo asked.

"I'm finishing a rug," *Tía* Meche replied. She took the small rug from the loom and stretched it on the floor.

"Awesome!" said Reynaldo. "I didn't know you could weave a roadrunner!"

"Roadrunners bring good luck!" she said, smiling. "I hope this weaving brings me good luck at the market on Saturday."

"Do they really bring good luck?" Reynaldo asked.

"*Sí*, my son. The old people say it's good to have a roadrunner around the house. Did you know they help keep the snakes and lizards away?"

Reynaldo looked at the old family loom *Abuelo* had fixed for him. If only he could make beautiful weavings like his aunt's, he thought to himself. He had made several practice pieces, but each time the stitches were loose and the edges had huge loops. *Tía* Meche told him that weaving takes skill, patience, and lots of practice.

"What are you going to weave today?" *Tía* Meche asked.

"Stripes!" Reynaldo cried. "I had a dream last night that my rug won a prize at the market this year."

"What a beautiful dream, Reynaldo," said *Tía* Meche, hugging him.

Reynaldo ran over to the old cabinet where *Tía* Meche kept the wool. He picked out the most brightly colored yarn spools he could find. Then he went outside to the courtyard to get some of the "bug red" yarn. Slowly, like his aunt had taught him,

he began to wind the colorful yarn onto a spool.

Reynaldo had an idea. Today, instead of using his new shuttle, he would use *Tía* Meche's old battered shuttle. He slowly began to weave one row after another.

Maybe it *was* magic! Before he knew it, Reynaldo's hands were moving quickly, just like *Tía* Meche's did. The old shuttle whizzed across the warp threads.

If only my *abuelo* were alive and could see me weave, Reynaldo thought, he would be proud of me. Reynaldo missed his grandfather very much, and tears filled his eyes.

The next morning, Reynaldo woke up very early. It was still dark outside, but he jumped out of bed and dressed quickly. He hurried to the workshop and turned on the lights. He continued to weave one row after another on his rug. Maybe it was *Tía* Meche's magical shuttle, because before long, Reynaldo had finished weaving his small rug.

> If you were to tell your parents about this story, what would you tell them about what you have read so far?

It was his best weaving ever—tight stitches, clean edges, and striking stripes!

"You look happy, Reynaldo," his aunt said when she entered the workshop.

"I finished my rug!" Reynaldo cried. "Now I can enter 'Magic Stripes' in the market competition!"

"*¡Qué lindo,* Reynaldo! How beautiful!" cried *Tía* Meche as she hugged him. "Weaving is in *your* blood, too."

As the morning sun made its way over the tall peaks of the mountains, Reynaldo and *Tía* Meche made their way toward the *placita,* carrying baskets full of weavings.

Tables were set around the plaza. *Tía* Meche and Reynaldo reached their table and began to unpack the colorful weavings.

After Reynaldo finished helping his aunt, he took "Magic Stripes" and entered his weaving in the contest. He carefully printed his name on the entry card.

The village was filling with people. They were strolling around the *placita,* looking at each artist's work. Tables, row after row, were stacked with bright weavings, *retablo*

C7

paintings, carvings, pottery, tinwork, and much more.

Kids were laughing and running around the *placita's* fountain. People were talking. And the *mariachis* were tuning their guitars.

When Reynaldo returned to his aunt's stall, he found a crowd of people gathered around, looking at *Tía* Meche's weavings. He pushed his way through and stood by his aunt.

"Have you ever seen a roadrunner woven on a rug before?" one woman asked.

"That Meche is so clever," another woman said.

"I'll take the rug with the roadrunner," shouted a man from behind. He pushed his way up front and handed *Tía* Meche some bills.

A man's voice came over the loudspeaker. It was time for the awards ceremony. He invited everyone to gather by the stage.

"I am pleased to announce that this year's first-place winner is 'Magic Stripes,'" he said. "Will the winner please come forward?"

Everyone began to clap. Reynaldo made his way up on stage. The judge smiled as he handed Reynaldo a big blue ribbon and an envelope with his prize—a check for $200! The judge asked Reynaldo to hold up

"Magic Stripes" for everyone to see. Amongst the crowd of people cheering, Reynaldo saw his family proudly looking at him.

Reynaldo ran down from the stage and hugged them all.

"Didn't I tell you that weaving is in your blood?" asked *Tía* Meche.

"Thank you, *Tía*," Reynaldo said as he kissed his aunt. "My dream came true!"

A photographer from the local newspaper took Reynaldo's photograph. The photograph and story, she said, would appear in Sunday's newspaper.

Would you recommend this story to a friend to read? Why or why not?

Yet Reynaldo felt something was missing. If only *Abuelo* could be here, too. But then knowing *Abuelo*, Reynaldo thought to himself and smiled, *Abuelo* probably already knows!"  ◉

## Living Legends

What adult in your life do you most admire? Reynaldo obviously admires his *Tía* Meche for her weaving skills as well as for her patience with him. Write a poem for the adult in your life who inspires you to become a better person. Illustrate your poem using the bright colors that might be in one of *Tía* Meche's rugs.

## Natural Talents

Everyone is born with certain talents. Some people are naturally good at math; some are born artists, musicians, or athletes; and others have a knack for making people laugh. Think of something you're good at, and imagine yourself making a living by using that particular skill. Write a few sentences about how you would train for that job.

## Traditions

Traditions are events, behaviors, or customs that occur over and over again and are passed from one generation to another. In Reynaldo's family, weaving is a family tradition. Many families have other kinds of traditions, like special meals served on special occasions. Schools have traditions, too. Many schools hold an annual food drive to help the needy. Think of a tradition you are involved in or know about. Use descriptive details to write about this tradition. If you know how the tradition started, be sure to share that information.

These days, it might seem as if a last name is optional, especially if you are famous. Chances are, you recognize the names *Cher, Madonna, Sting,* and *Elvis* without their last names. But most of us aren't so well known—our last names are an important way we identify ourselves.

People didn't always use last names. When communities consisted of just a few people, last names weren't important. But as towns grew, and more and more people had the same names, it became important to tell them apart. The Chinese were the first people to adopt *surnames,* or last names, to honor their ancestors. However, they place the surname first. For example, the surname of *Sun Yat-sen* is *Sun.*

The first surnames came from many sources. Often people were named for their occupations, whether they were *Carpenters, Taylors, Bakers,* or *Masons.* Place names were common, too. Have you ever met someone with the last name of *Hill, Brook,* or *Forest?* Names were also used to identify people who moved from place to place. For example, a person from Wales was called *Walsh,* while the German name *Von Berger* means "from Berger."

Many last names were created to identify the person's parents or where the family was from. The common Scandinavian name *Johnson* means "son of John." Other countries adopted the same system. For example, we have the Scottish *MacDonald,* the Irish *O'Brien,* the Dutch *VanBuren,* the French *DeGaulle,* and the Italian *DiTello.*

What do you know about *your* family name? What does it mean? To find out, check out a Web site such as www.nameseekers.co.uk/surname.htm. Happy digging, and be sure to share what you learn with your family.

# THEY CALL HER Maria

## BY PATRICIA ALMADA

Have you ever built a playhouse? When Maria Montoya was eight years old, she built her first *adobe* playhouse with her younger sister Desideria. Every spring after that, the girls built bigger houses, using only mud and clay to make the bricks, as they had seen the people of their *pueblo* do so many times before. Inside, the girls built fireplaces with chimneys, but they were never allowed to light them. Their playhouse had two rooms, one for each of their imaginary families.

As they played house, the girls took good care of the dolls their mother had made for them. Maria's doll was a gray rabbit skin stuffed with dry grasses and decorated with red fabric patches for the eyes and mouth. Desideria's doll was very different—just an ear of red corn with green painted eyes and a mouth.

Using small *metates* (flat stones to grind corn) they pretended to make tortillas for their dolls and for the other children who came to visit.

> How are Maria and her sister Desideria like you? How are they different from you?

Every day the girls swept the house using brooms made by their father: a soft sagebrush broom for inside and a stiffer rabbit brush broom for the ground outside. Their mother used seven different brooms in their home, but two were plenty for the playhouse!

One day Maria decided to make dishes of her own for the playhouse. Before gathering clay at the irrigation ditch, she sprinkled a little blue cornmeal on the ground to give thanks to Mother Earth for the gift of the clay, as the older women always did. Maria and Desideria then molded small bowls and jars and set them out to dry. The next day they discovered that everything had cracked in the sun. So they went to visit Aunt Nicolasa for advice. Aunt Nicolasa's pottery was admired by all in the *pueblo*.

Aunt Nicolasa knew that the best way for the girls to learn was by watching her. So the girls sat quietly by their aunt's side as she mixed dry clay, sand, and water; kneaded it for a long time; and made it into a ball. Then Aunt Nicolasa patted the clay to form the bottom of a pot. Next she rolled snake-like ropes of clay between the palms of her hands and coiled them one by one around the flat base. Finally, she smoothed and blended the pot with great care.

Aunt Nicolasa gave each girl a chunk of clay and let them make their own pots. Aunt Nicolasa explained to the girls that pottery-making belonged to all of the women in the *pueblo*, with one woman teaching the next, so that each generation would benefit from the one before it. Little did they know at the time that Maria would grow up to become a world-famous potter.

"MY MOTHER DIDN'T DO POTTERY, SO I LEARNED IT FROM MY AUNT.

**Step 1:** Mix dry clay, sand, and water. Then knead it into a ball.

**Step 2:** Roll a piece of clay into a snake-like rope.

**Step 3:** Coil the clay ropes around the flat base.

Remembering those early days, Maria said, "My mother didn't do pottery, so I learned it from my aunt. I just learned it for myself. I learned it with my whole heart."

Pottery in Maria's *pueblo* of San Ildefonso was made only in the summer, when the days were warm and the air dry. In the fall, Maria and her sister went to school, first in the *pueblo* and then to a faraway boarding school in Santa Fe. Being away from home was difficult for Maria because she missed her family, the traditions of the village, and working with clay. She was anxious to go home once her two years at the boarding school ended.

At 17, Maria fell in love and married Julian Martinez. The Indian Agency hired the young couple, along with other members of the *pueblo*, to demonstrate songs, dances, crafts, and foods at the St. Louis World's Fair.

People from all over the world watched Maria shape pots before their eyes. By now Maria had become an excellent potter. But Maria was shy among so many strangers and so, once again, she was happy to go home.

New beginnings awaited Julian and Maria at the *pueblo*. Julian went to work in the fields and Maria prepared for the birth of their first son, Adam.

Two years later, a daughter, Yellow Pond Lily, was born, but Maria's joy was mixed with sadness because hard times had come to the *pueblo*. A frost had destroyed the crops. Then a long drought was followed by rains that flooded the land. The people suffered, food was limited, and the men were forced to find work outside the *pueblo*. Julian was hired by an archaeological team

What is the most interesting thing you have learned so far in this article?

"I JUST LEARNED IT FOR MYSELF. I LEARNED IT WITH MY WHOLE HEART."

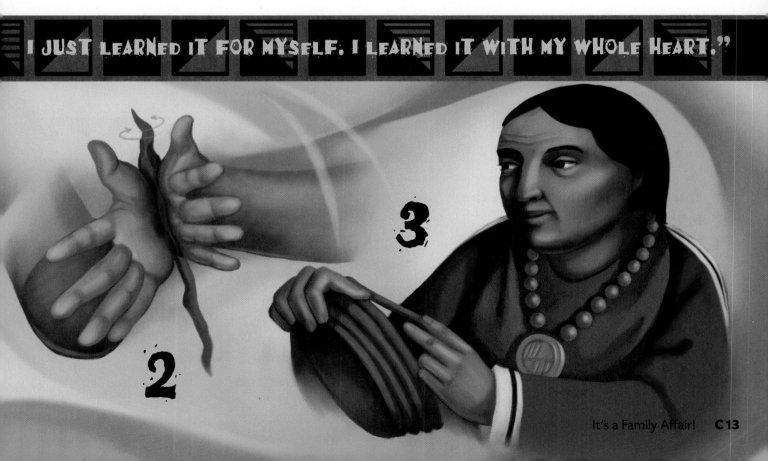

2

3

Julian did the painting. The archaeologist was delighted with the results. He bought all the pieces the couple had finished and ordered more. A great demand for Maria's pottery began when her work was displayed in a museum gift shop in Santa Fe. Maria's most famous style became her "black-on-black" pottery—pieces that were slowly smoked in the firing pit until the red clay turned black. When parts of the pot were polished before the firing, they became shiny black, but the unpolished sections were matte, or dull black. The dull and shiny contrast was stunning.

that was conducting a dig. When they saw that he could draw well, he was asked to copy the ancient designs found at the dig. Maria's pottery skills also caught the eye of an archaeologist. He suggested that the couple work together to make a copy of a pot based on a small shard found at the dig.

So Maria and Julian started making pottery together. Maria shaped the clay and

Maria shared her success with her family and friends in the *pueblo* by teaching others and encouraging them to sell their pottery along with hers. The entire *pueblo* gained from the popularity of Maria's pots.

Along with Julian, many family members helped in the effort. They were involved in

WHAT LARGE STEPS SHE DID TAKE. THE COURAGE UNMEASURABLE.

# MARIA

**You can see Maria's work at the following museums:**

♦ American Museum of Natural History, New York City

♦ Museum of New Mexico, Santa Fe

♦ Museum of Northern Arizona, Flagstaff

♦ Smithsonian Institution, Washington, DC

♦ Southwest Museum, Los Angeles

collecting, mixing, and kneading the clay; and in scraping, sanding, polishing, decorating, and firing the pots. New generations of gifted artists were trained at Maria's side. Maria's sons, Adam and Popovi Da, became well known for their creative styles, and the gift of pottery-making was passed on to their children and grandchildren as well.

To her great niece, Barbara Gonzalez, Maria said, "When I am gone, essentially other people have my pots. But to you I leave my greatest achievement, which is the ability to do it." Barbara, in turn, speaks of her love and admiration for Maria with these words: "What large steps you did take. The courage unmeasurable. My pace so slow . . . I can never catch up."

Maria Martinez, the humble woman from San Ildefonso, made beautiful pottery for over 70 years. She was proud of her ancestry, always wearing traditional Native American clothing wherever she went. The once shy young woman became at ease among artists, presidents, and art critics, but she was always happiest in the *pueblo*, with her large family. Maria continued to make beautiful pottery until she was ninety-one years old.

Maria's life was not an easy one—she outlived her baby daughter, two sons, and her husband, Julian. She knew hunger and bad times, but she worked hard and helped many people along the way. She passed away in 1980, at the age of ninety-seven. Many of her descendants continue to make pottery today.

Synthesize the life of Maria Martinez in three sentences. Share your synthesis with a friend.

**Left:** Maria teaching a class of students, including her family.

**Right:** These are examples of Maria and her family's pottery.

## SIMPLE FUN

Sometimes the simplest things bring the most joy. When Maria and her sister Desideria were small, their favorite toys were simple ones made from household materials. Did you ever have a similar toy? Perhaps you made a fort out of a giant cardboard box, spent an afternoon making paper airplanes, or giggled with your friends over Chinese jump rope or a homemade craft. Write a journal entry about why your simple toy was so much fun.

## THE GREATEST GIFT

Toward the end of her life, Maria talked about her greatest achievement. Perhaps you were surprised that she did not mention creating beautiful pottery for her customers to enjoy. What was your reaction to her statement? How does her attitude show her strong sense of family? Discuss your ideas with a classmate.

## FAMILY TALENT TREE

Maria became an excellent potter because her family encouraged her to follow her dreams. She also inherited some talent from her aunt. Chances are, you're good at something—whether it's art, math, science, or cooking. Think of your best talent and how you developed it. Who has helped you develop this talent? Write an ad to advertise your talent. Be sure to include information about how you became so good at this talent.

# Creating a Class Yearbook

Some families have a family photo album that holds photos from family events, newspaper articles from historical events, and stories that tell about family members. Your class is like your family at school. So create a class yearbook to share all that's happened over the year.

## What you'll need:

- A scrapbook or blank book.
- Photos from class events, if available.
- Scrapbooking supplies, such as markers to write down class stories, tape or glue to make your photos stick, and stickers for decorating. Be sure to use products that are safe for photos.

## How to start:

- Think back through the events of the school year. What events stick out in your mind the most? Why? Find photos or any other keepsakes that go with these events.
- Think about your classmates. Who are your friends? Why are they so special to you? Are there funny or sad stories about your classmates that you want to remember? Find or take photos of your classmates.
- Did anything important happen in United States history during the school year? What was it? How did you feel about that historical event? Find magazine or newspaper articles about the event.
- Think about your teacher. How did your teacher help you during the school year? What are things that you will always remember about your teacher? Find or take a photo of your teacher.
- Think about one story that you would like to leave behind for the incoming class next year. What is it about? Why would you want next year's class to know about this story?

Once you've thought about these things and you've gathered photos and any other keepsakes, begin your yearbook. Be sure to write down all the stories that you want to remember about your class. You'll have a blast looking back on your yearbook over the years.

## SYNTHESIZING

# Hey! Read This Blurb!

When you go to the library or bookstore, how do you choose which book to read? Many people rely on what's written on book jackets and back covers to find out what a book is about. That's where you usually find a synthesis of the plot, a description of the main characters, and perhaps information about the writer's style.

This piece of text is called a *blurb,* because it's short and informative. Authors and publishers **synthesize** the book in order to attract readers. They highlight important parts of the book in the blurb, giving readers reasons to buy or borrow the book.

Take a few minutes to look back at some of the book jackets or back covers on books you've recently read, including a book that you didn't particularly like. Would you synthesize the book in the same way the authors and publishers did?

Remember, synthesizing means taking pieces of information from what you've read and combining them with your background knowledge in order to better understand the book. When we synthesize, we may form a new idea about the book we just read.

Synthesizing reflects our own personal reaction to whatever we've read, and it leaves room for others to agree or disagree with us. So remember, after reading a book, it's OK to find out that you don't always agree with the synthesis on the book jacket or back cover. That's what makes reading such a personal experience.

Read This!

Freedom

Austin is sure his summer vacation is going to be boring. He has a broken arm and he can't play ball, ride his bike, or do much of anything. But all this changes when he spots an eagle— an eagle he calls Skyrider.

# A Walk in the Woods

by Diane Bair and Pamela Wright

Let's go hunting—with our eyes! You can learn a lot about animals by observing their behaviors. If you watch closely, you may discover what they eat, where they sleep, and how they raise their young. Let's spend some time with two animal families: a pair of bald eagles and their two eaglets, and a mother black bear and her two cubs. How are these two families alike? How are they different?

## Day One with the Eagles

We look through a telescope along the coast of Maine. We spot a bald eagle perched on a tall branch. The snow-white head and cotton-colored tail feathers show brightly against the dark-colored body of this grown eagle. Its large, pale eyes are set on the rocky coastline and surrounding wetlands. Its long, hooked beak shines golden yellow. Sharp, black talons curl around the tree branch.

Suddenly, the eagle takes flight. Its wings spread wide, reaching across 6 feet or more. It catches the wind and soars high above the water.

Bald eagles are found throughout North America. They live near water. Among the largest birds in North America, they can grow more than 3 feet tall from beak to tail and have wingspans up to 8 feet. They can fly up to 75 miles per hour and as fast as 200 miles per hour when they dive for food.

What is the most interesting thing you have learned about eagles so far?

Although the number of bald eagles living in America is increasing, they are still threatened animals.

## Day One with the Bears

We crouch beneath towering pine trees that overlook a meadow of wildflowers and berry bushes. We are in the deep, dark woods of Minnesota. Crunch. Crunch. We hear heavy steps on the forest floor. Crack. A tree branch breaks and the sound echoes in the forest. We watch as a large bear shuffles out of the woods, followed by two look-alike cubs. Quietly, we lift our binoculars to get a closer peek.

The mother's huge body is covered in thick, shaggy black fur. She has a large head, small rounded ears, and tiny eyes. The cubs are miniatures of their mother— little black furballs. We watch as the adult rubs her back against the trunk of a tree, leaving patches of fur stuck in the bark, and lifts her head toward us. Quickly, she scampers away and the cubs go running and tumbling after her.

Black bears are the most common bears in North America. They live in forests and wooded mountain areas. They grow to be about 5 to 6 feet long. Male black bears can weigh 130 to 600 pounds. Adult female bears usually weigh 90 to 300 pounds. They are fast climbers—as fast as squirrels—and can run up to 40 miles per hour. They also have an excellent sense of smell.

Maybe that's why they ran away so fast! They got a whiff of us!

## Day Two with the Eagles

Today we spotted the eagles' nest! It is the largest bird's nest we have ever seen, measuring almost 5 feet wide and 4 feet deep. It sits atop a tall tree on the edge of the ocean. There are two eagles in the area. One is always on the nest. The other is either perched on a nearby tree or in search of food. With binoculars, we can see two eaglets in the nest.

Eagles mate for life, and both the male and female share the responsibilities of raising their young. Eagles use the same nest year after year, adding new twigs and branches each year. Eagle nests can be 6 feet wide, 5 feet deep, and weigh as much as a small car!

The female lays from one to three eggs in early spring. This may take several days. The eggs hatch 35 days later. Once the eggs hatch, the female guards them constantly, while the male provides food for the family. Later, as the chicks grow, the female will help with the hunting, too. Eagles feed their young by shredding pieces of meat and offering them these tiny morsels.

## Day Two with the Bears

The playful, energetic cubs are always with their mother. They tag along wherever she goes. Black bear cubs are usually born in January and February while the mother is in hibernation. When they are first born, they are blind and weigh only about three quarters of a pound! Black bears generally have two to three cubs. Twins are common. A mother black bear will have babies about every two or three years. The father bear does not help raise the cubs.

The mother and her cubs leave the den in early spring. The cubs stay with their mother throughout the first year. They learn how to find food, where to sleep, and when and where to seek shelter from danger.

> What is the most interesting thing you have learned about bears so far?

## Day Three with the Eagles

The eagle looks as if it is floating in the air, hovering high above the tallest treetops. It glides along in the air. We notice that the eagle rarely flaps its wings like other birds. In a quick motion, it swoops down into the water, snatching a small fish with its sharp talons. The fish dangles in the eagle's clasp as the bird soars out of view.

Eagles are raptors. This means that they hunt and eat live prey. They hunt for fish and other small animals and birds.

Eagles have binocular vision. This means that they can see things faraway, which allows them to spot prey while they are flying. Eagles' eyes can move separately, too, giving them a wide range of vision. One eye can look to the left while the other eye looks to the right. It's like having two periscopes!

## Day Three with the Bears

Today we watch as the mother teaches her cubs what to eat and where to find food. We see them most often during early morning or in the evening, when they are looking for food. First, they nibble on plants and grasses. Later, all three bears feast on the wild raspberries growing along the edge of the forest. They also eat berries, plants, insects, fish, and dead animals.

Suddenly, the mother bear stands on her hind legs, pawing the trunk of a tree. What is she doing? Later, we notice scratch marks on the bark made by the bear's five claws. Bears like to eat the sweet layer under tree bark called *cambium*.

## Day Four with the Eagles

We see only one eaglet. The other is gone. Perhaps it has fallen from the nest. Maybe its older sibling has killed it. This is not uncommon.

The eaglet is covered in a coat of gray down. In a few weeks, it will begin to grow black feathers. Bald eagles' heads and tails do not turn white until they are four or five years old.

Eagles grow quickly, adding a pound every four or five days. At three weeks old, they are a foot tall. At six weeks, they are nearly as big as their parents.

Soon the parents will begin teaching the eaglet to fly. The eaglet will take its first flight when it is about ten to thirteen weeks old. Throughout the summer, it will also learn to hunt for its own food. By winter, the young eagle will leave the nesting area and its parents. Twenty weeks or so after hatching, it is on its own.

Good luck, little eagle!

## Day Four with the Bears

The cubs are maturing so fast! The young cubs play in the river, pawing and sipping the water. Their mother moves quickly along the riverbank, coaxing them along. They are heading to their favorite feeding area. Black bear mothers nurse their young for six to nine months. Between July and September of their first year, they switch to solid food.

By the end of the summer, the cubs are not yet ready to leave their mother. The family will spend the first winter together. They will even sleep through the cubs' first birthday. But by their second winter, the cubs will be on their own.

Good luck, little cubs! ○

> Would you recommend this article to a friend to read? Why or why not?

### Eagles
- Endangered animals in North America
- Live near water
- Fly as fast as 75 mph, 200 mph when diving
- Can grow up to 3 feet tall
- Eat fish, birds, and small animals
- Excellent sense of sight
- Lay one to three eggs
- Young hatch in early spring
- The mother and father help raise the young
- Eaglets leave their parents at twenty weeks of age

### Bears
- Common species in North America
- Live in wooded areas
- Run as fast as 40 mph
- Can grow up to 6 feet long
- Eat plants, grasses, and berries
- Excellent sense of smell
- Give birth to two or three cubs
- Young born in winter
- The mother raises the young on her own
- Cubs leave their mother after one year

# Stop and Respond

## Make a Choice

Which animal did you find more interesting—the bald eagle or the black bear? Use details from the article to write a paragraph supporting your choice. For example, your paragraph might include facts or descriptive details that surprised you.

## Naturalist's Notebook

What's your favorite animal? How might this animal look to you if you watched it in the wilderness? Gather lots of details by collecting information from science books or animal field guides. Write a journal entry about what you might see. Use the authors' style from "A Walk in the Woods" as a model.

## A Walk to Remember

Think of a time when you took a nature walk in the woods, on the beach, or in a local park. Create a poster that describes the wildlife and plants that you saw. Include information about the sights, sounds, and smells that you experienced on your walk so that your reader can imagine being there with you.

# The Wedding

by Angela Shelf Medearis

My mom put bright red hearts on the calendar and smiled at me.

"Only two weeks left until the wedding, Mark," she said happily.

Two double hearts marked the date of the wedding, September 30th. It was no use telling her again that I wasn't happy about the fact that she was getting remarried. I told her when she first started dating Gerald Reeves that I didn't need another father. I had hoped that somehow my mom and dad would get back together. They divorced when I was in kindergarten. That was five years ago.

Recently, my dad got married again and moved away to Colorado. He sent photographs of his new wife the other day. Looking at the photographs made me feel sad. I knew then that there wasn't a chance that my mom and dad would ever get back together.

I especially hated the idea that Gerald and his two teenage sons, Rodney and Kenneth, would be moving into our house. Everyone tries hard to make me feel like part of the family, but I don't. Rodney and Kenneth really love Mom and they're always hanging around in the kitchen when they're visiting us. The kitchen used to be the place where Mom and I hung out and talked. Now it seems crowded. I usually just stay in my room when Gerald and his sons come over.

The other day, they were all playing basketball out in the driveway, just like my dad and I used to do. Gerald saw me looking at them from the window and told me to come down and play. I told him I had homework to do.

What have you learned about Mark so far?

"Mark, I need you on my team," Gerald said, smiling. "These guys are killing me. Come on—together we'll be unbeatable."

"OK," I said finally.

Gerald and I beat them, and he gave me a big hug at the end of the game. I had fun, but it really made me miss my dad.

This whole marriage thing is confusing to me. How can people be married and happy one minute and sad and divorced the next? I just don't get it.

"Let's go, Mark," Mom said, interrupting my thoughts. "I need to photocopy the wedding program."

We were driving down the street to the photocopy store when I saw Logan. I waved as we went by.

Logan and I used to be good friends. But lately, he seems to always be at soccer or swimming practice. We don't get to hang out together like we used to.

"Did I tell you that I want you to give me away at the wedding?" Mom asked.

"What do you mean?" I asked.

"You'll walk me down the aisle, give my hand to Gerald's, give him a hug, shake hands with his sons, and go and sit down."

"What if I don't want to give you away?" I asked.

"Well, you don't have to if you don't want to," Mom said. She looked kind of disappointed. "But Gerald and I both want all our sons to be a part of the ceremony."

"I'll think about it," I said.

Our next stop was the tuxedo shop.

"May I help you?" the salesman asked.

"No," I said.

"Yes," Mom said. "Don't be so disagreeable, Mark."

The salesman looked confused.

"Look, Mom," I said, "I'll go to the wedding, but I don't know if I want to give you away or not."

"Mark," Mom said, "I'm not trying to push you into anything, but if you're going to walk me down the aisle, you'll need to wear a tuxedo."

"Do I have to make up my mind now?" I asked.

"The wedding is in two weeks," Mom said. "We have to order the tuxedo today."

"Well, I don't know if I want to be a part of the wedding yet," I said. "I need more time to think about it."

"I thought you liked Gerald," Mom said.

"He's always nice to me," I said. "He's just not my dad."

"Gerald's not trying to replace your dad," Mom said.

"I know that," I said. "I like Gerald, Rodney, and Kenneth. I just don't like the fact that I have to share you with them."

"I thought you approved of our marriage," Mom said. "I thought you were looking forward to us all becoming a family."

"I don't know what to think," I said. "I need some more time."

"Well, time is the one thing we don't have a lot of," Mom said.

"Excuse me," the salesman said. "Perhaps I can help. We can take his measurements and order the tux. If you decide not to use it, all you have to do is give me a call."

Mom and I looked at each other. She looked so sad that for a minute, I almost wanted to tell the salesman that we'd be taking the tuxedo. But I didn't.

"That's fine," Mom said. "I'll call you by Saturday morning and let you know if we'll need it."

We were both quiet on the way home. Logan was still outside, kicking his soccer ball against the side of his house.

"Let me out here, OK?" I said. "I'm going to talk to Logan for awhile."

"Be home by six o'clock," Mom said. "Gerald and the boys are moving their things in tonight. We'll need your help."

"OK," I said.

"What's up with you?" Logan asked. "Where were you?"

"We had stuff to do for the wedding," I said.

"What wedding?" Logan asked.

"My mom's marrying Gerald Reeves. The wedding is in two weeks."

"Gerald Reeves, the basketball coach at Winston High School?" Logan asked.

"Yes," I said. "Do you know his sons, Kenneth and Rodney?"

What do you think Mark will talk to Logan about? What earlier events helped you to make that prediction?

"They were my camp counselors last summer!" Logan said. "They're great at soccer and basketball, too! I can't believe that they're going to be living down the street. You're *so* lucky."

"Why am I so lucky?"

"Because you're going to have three of the most amazing guys in the world as part of your family."

We kicked the ball back and forth several times. I kept thinking about what Logan had said. Gerald, Kenneth, and Rodney *were* nice. My mom was the happiest she'd been in years. So why was I feeling so sad? Suddenly I knew who I needed to talk to.

As soon as I got home, I took the telephone into my room and called my dad. We talked for an hour about everything. I guess I'd never really wanted to talk about the divorce before.

"Look, Mark," Dad said, "just keep a level head about all this. The main thing you need to remember is that now you're a part of *two* families that love you. You're lucky. Some people only have one."

"Thanks, Dad," I said.

"Sharie wants to talk to you," Dad said. "There's something she wants to ask you."

Then Dad's new wife got on the phone. She invited me to come visit them over our winter break. I told her I would if it was fine with Mom and Gerald. After all, I told her, this would be the first vacation from

school that we'd be together as a family. We said goodbye and I went to look for Mom. She was trying on her wedding dress.

"You look great, Mom," I said.

"Thanks, Mark," she said. "I know all this has been hard for you."

"I think I've been making things harder than they really are," I said. "Is the tuxedo shop still open?"

"Yes," Mom said, "it's open until nine o'clock."

"Good," I said. "Can you call them? I'll need that tuxedo when I give you away. I don't want to be the only one in the wedding party who's not dressed up!"

> Who would you recommend this story to? Why do you think that person would enjoy reading this story?

### Being a Good Friend

Imagine that Mark is your friend. You know that he is confused and upset about the changes that are happening in his family. In a letter, list three pieces of advice you would have for your friend.

### Two Points of View

The upcoming wedding of Mark's mother created a variety of different feelings: joy, excitement, anger, and even envy. Choose two characters in the story and compare their attitudes about Mark's new family. Use a compare-and-contrast chart to record your ideas.

### Attitude Is Everything

As Mark talks to his father, he realizes that his attitude about his mother's wedding has made the situation more difficult than it has to be. Sometimes that's the way it is when we face major changes. Think of a situation in which that might be the case—it could be a move to another town, a fight with a friend, or even the loss of a pet. Write a story outline that shows a character's problem and how the story was resolved.

# Let's Write

## Family Biographer

Interview an older person. Get information on the person's date and place of birth and the major events in his or her life. Your questions might focus on what it was like growing up during a particular time period. You might also focus on what the person's happiest memory is or what games he or she played as a child. Write a one-page biography about the person and share it with the class.

## Pull Up a Chair and I'll Tell You a Story

Is there a story that a family member, friend, or neighbor has told you so many times that now you can tell the story yourself? Think of a story that you have heard over and over again and retell it in your own words. Make your story as interesting as you can. Include important details about the people in the story and what happened to them. Give your story a title and share it with the class.

## Customs From Around the World

Many families and cultures have traditions or customs that are important to them. Family traditions might include things like having corned beef and cabbage on St. Patrick's Day. A German custom is to hide a pickle ornament on the Christmas tree. Do some research on the Internet or look in the library for books that talk about customs around the world. Find an interesting custom or tradition and create a "Did You Know" poster that explains this custom or tradition to your classmates.

## More Books

Douglas, Ann. *The Family Tree Detective: Cracking the Case of Your Family's Story.* Owl Communications, 1999.

Flegg, Jim. *Little Wonders: Animal Families (Wild World).* Millbrook Press, 1991.

Willard, Jim. *Ancestors: A Beginner's Guide to Family History and Geneology.* Houghton Mifflin, 1997.

## On the Web

**Discover Animals**
http://www.animal.discovery.com
http://www.enature.com

**Bird Watching**
http://www.wildbirds.com

**Researching Your Family**
http://www.geocities.com/enchantedforest/
     5283/genekids.htm

## Across the Curriculum

### Art

Find some colorful scrap paper, like wrapping paper, magazine pictures, or construction paper. Cut the paper into strips that are 1 inch wide by 12 inches long. Lay six strips onto a sheet of background paper. Leave about 1 inch between strips. Glue only the ends of the strips down to the background paper. Then take your remaining strips and begin weaving in and out in the opposite direction of the strips on the background paper. Continue weaving until you've finished your pattern. Use your weaving as a place mat or as a wall hanging.

### Social Studies

Write a letter to a family member or neighbor asking them about their personal experience of a historical event, such as the first moon walk, the outbreak of a war, or a major weather emergency. Ask them to recall what they were doing when they first found out about the event, how they reacted to it, and how the event affected their lives. You might also ask them whether their attitude about the event has changed over the years. Ask them to write back to you with their thoughts. Talk with a classmate about your letters.

# And the Answer Is...!

The families described in *It's a Family Affair!* have some things in common, but they have many differences, too. Here's a fun game to play with your classmates—a guessing game that tests your knowledge about the families in this issue! Work with a partner and see how many of these questions you can answer.

1. What is the Spanish word for *Aunt*?
2. Which family loves to eat berries, plants, fish, and dead animals?
3. Who has a daughter named Yellow Pond Lily?
4. How many stepbrothers will Mark inherit when his mom remarries?
5. What were the occupations of Reynaldo's parents?
6. In which two families is creating art a family tradition?
7. How does Mark's dad help Mark feel better about his mom's upcoming wedding?
8. Members of which family are considered an endangered species?
9. A childhood activity with her sister Desideria inspired Maria Martinez' life's work. What was it?
10. What family member does Reynaldo hope to make proud with his rug weaving?

COMPREHENSION QUARTERLY

# CQ⁴

**ISSUE D:** Inferring

# Good Job

# Good Job!

**THINK ABOUT:** Inferring

**D4**

FICTION
## Pony Rider
Don't be fooled by Danny's appearance—there's a lot more to this pony wrangler than meets the eye!

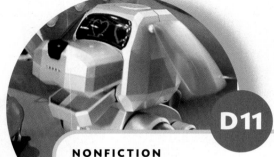

**D11**

NONFICTION
## Robots to the Rescue
Robots can do everything that humans can do—or can they?

**D18**

FICTION
## Lemonade for Sale
A lemonade sale gets out of hand when a lot more than lemonade is sold.

**D24**

NONFICTION
## The "Who" and Even the "Oops!"
Ordinary people find inventive, and sometimes amusing, ways to make life a little easier.

## In this issue:

### INFERRING

# Crime Goes to Work

If you're wondering where Shanti is, look in the beanbag chair in the corner of the family room. She's probably curled up there with her nose poked into a book. Shanti reads every chance she gets—usually mysteries, her favorite genre. She always tries to solve a mystery before the detective does, and she's read so many mysteries and searched for so many clues that she usually succeeds.

Like all good readers, Shanti makes frequent **inferences** as she reads. She thinks about what is happening in the book and connects it to what she already knows—her background knowledge. She compares characters' actions with the way people act in real life and the twists and turns of the plot with experiences in her own life. That's how she comes up with interpretations that are hers alone. As she reads, Shanti draws conclusions and makes predictions about what will happen next, based on her inferences. As she reads on, Shanti revises her predictions whenever she needs to, based on new information in the text.

Right now, Shanti is making several inferences as she reads this passage from *Crime in the Cubicle,* which is a story about people in an office who are disappearing from a mysterious cubicle. What inferences can you make from the passage?

As Anna tiptoed into the cubicle, she heard a soft, rustling sound. *I'm so nervous, I'm hearing things,* she thought to herself. *I know everyone is downstairs at the office party. I saw them all there.*

Anna hated going anywhere near this cubicle. It was the one her pal John had entered and from which he had disappeared. But Anna was being her usual stubborn self and wasn't about to give up until she figured out what happened to her friend . . .

Think about making inferences as you read the articles in this issue. Try to connect the text with what you already know to form your own interpretations.

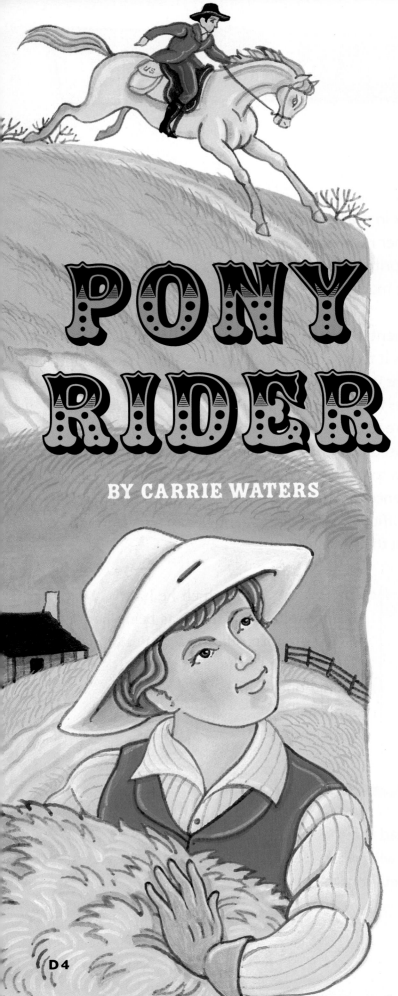

# PONY RIDER

## BY CARRIE WATERS

A wild coyote yell came from the east. Then Pa's voice rang from the shed roof. "Rider coming in!"

Danny dropped a hay bale and sprinted for the corral. A pinto pony was tied there. By the time the little filly's bit was in her mouth and her saddle tightened, the rider was skidding to a halt in the station yard. Danny hurried to lead the relief horse out. But the filly balked at the corral gate, set her front hooves, and refused to budge.

"Hey, skinny shanks! Get that mount over here, pronto!" Jake Carmmody trotted toward the corral, leading a palomino mare that was blowing and hanging her head. "Come on! Are you a wrangler or a chicken farmer?"

Had Jake always been this ornery, Danny wondered, or was he just full of himself since he'd started riding for the Pony Express? He couldn't be a day over fifteen.

"Hold it." Facing the filly, Danny walked backward, moving side to side, side to side. The horse turned her head to and fro, watching, and that threw her just enough off balance to make her take a step, then two.

Jake tossed the mail-filled mochilla over the saddle. "Good trick," he said, adjusting the specially made saddle bag. "Where'd you learn it?"

"I . . . from a girl I know."

"Girls!" Jake said. He spat in the dirt. "Useless. Tell your pa that horse needs doctoring." He pointed at two deep scratches on the palomino's flank.

"What happened?" Danny asked.

"There was a cougar at Granite Rock," Jake said. "Oh, I almost forgot." He tossed a leather packet in Danny's direction. "That's for your pa." He stood before the injured horse, lifted her head, looked in her eyes, and saluted smartly, just like a soldier.

"Why'd you do that?" Danny asked.

"Because she's a brave little lady," Jake answered. He leaped onto the fresh horse. "Take good care of her."

"I will," Danny said.

But Jake was already galloping out of the yard and away.

What kind of a person do you think Jake is? What information in the text did you use to decide this?

They had rabbit stew and hominy grits with molasses for supper that night. Pa pointed at Danny's head. "Hat," he said. "I declare, you're acting more like a mannerless boy every day, Danielle Foster."

"Wasn't that the idea?" Grinning, Danny tugged her hat off. Two fat golden braids tumbled out onto her shoulders. "Jake Carmmody told me yesterday that I run like a girl," she said, "if that makes you feel any better."

Pa narrowed his eyes at her. "It doesn't," he said.

Danny dug into her stew. "Don't worry, Pa," she said. "Nobody is going to find out." Pa needed this job with the Overland Pony Express. He was as fine a horseman as ever lived, and with the money from this job, he finally had a chance to start that horse ranch he'd been dreaming about.

Pa was trying hard not to grin. "Well, I will say, those trousers and that big shirt don't show off your beauty." Hank Foster

wasn't sure whether the company would officially allow a man to bring his eleven-year-old daughter to a swing station, but Danielle was with him. Period. So he hadn't asked.

Danny was smoothing out the newspaper ad nailed up on the log wall of their cabin.

Were you surprised to discover that Danny is a girl? What clues in the text might have helped you to guess this?

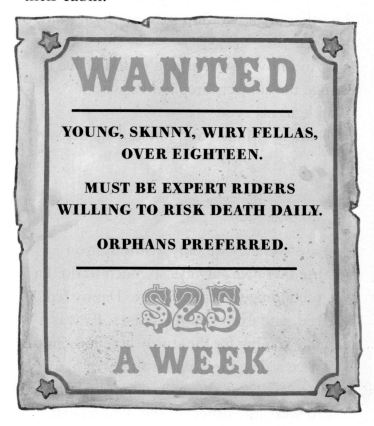

WANTED

YOUNG, SKINNY, WIRY FELLAS, OVER EIGHTEEN.

MUST BE EXPERT RIDERS WILLING TO RISK DEATH DAILY.

ORPHANS PREFERRED.

$25 A WEEK

"I'm just as good a rider as any of these pony boys," Danny said.

"I believe you are," Pa answered.

Danny added, "And I'd sure like to change that Jake Carmmody's opinion of girls."

Pa shook his head. "Danielle . . ."

"What was in that leather pouch?" she quickly asked.

"Danielle, you're changing the subject."

Danielle nodded and took a big bite of stew.

Pa watched his daughter before answering her question. "It was just company business. A company director and some bigwig state senator from Missouri are coming out to inspect the station sometime next week. We need to be shipshape for the visitors. About Carmmody . . ."

"You're always shipshape, Pa. Some of the other swing-station men are living out of tents."

"And now you're trying to flatter me to change the subject," replied Pa with a twinkle in his eyes.

Danielle grinned and nodded again.

Days went by quickly at the station because there was always so much to do. Pa was rebuilding the corral fence. Danny fed, watered, and exercised the horses. Pa was a big man, too big for the sturdy little mustangs.

Twice a day, there was a flurry of activity as the riders came through, one traveling east to west, the other on the west to east run. Riders were supposed to change horses in 2 minutes or less, and at the Foster station they did.

Today, Carmmody was later than usual. Danny thought about his close call at Granite Rock and shivered. Then she heard Pa's shout of "Rider!" from the far side of the corral and ran for the relief horse. When she got back to the yard, Jake Carmmody

was there all right, but he was sitting in the dust shaking, and Pa was leaning over him.

"It's the fever," Pa told Danny.

"Help me up," Jake said. His words were slurred. "Tie me to the saddle." The Pony Express rider always got through, no matter what—everybody knew that. Out in the Territory, Josh Zowgaltz got hit with a dozen arrows and still managed to make it to the end of his run.

"You're not going anywhere, son," Pa told Jake.

"I'll go," Danny said. "It's only 14 miles to Home Station." Riders passed off the mail and stayed overnight there. "I can do it, Pa." In a flash, she was up in the saddle. She leaned down to take the mochilla from her pa, and her hat slipped. One braid fell down. The last thing she saw before wheeling the pony was Jake Carmmody, mouth open, staring.

Danny was grateful that it was the palomino she was riding. The horse was a steady mount, experienced on this run. Some of the horses were newly-caught mustangs with very little saddle training.

What do you predict will happen on Danny's ride? What makes you think this?

The first part of the ride was a steady climb up a narrow, rocky trail to Granite Rock. The right side of the trail fell away to a steep slope, but the palomino was surefooted. Up near the top of the hill was a big granite outcrop. Just in front of the rock, the palomino started dancing. She reared. That's when Danny saw it. The cougar, still as a statue, was crouched on the rock, golden eyes staring.

Danny heard her own pulse beating in her ears, and her back tingled with the thought of that big cat springing. She pulled back on the reins. The palomino backed up and stood skittishly, pawing the ground. "I don't blame you, girl," Danny said. "I feel the same way. But we're the Express, and we've got to get through." She took a deep breath and gave the loudest, screechingest Pony Express coyote yell she could muster. The palomino lunged forward, and Danny saw the big cat's tail disappear behind the rock.

Was your inference correct? If not, reread pages D4 and D5 to look for any clues you might have missed.

By the end of the day, Danny was trotting back toward home. From the hill above the station, she could see a wagon pulled up under a scrub tree. Two men in fancy clothes were standing beside it, talking with her pa. They were the important visitors. And in the corral saddling a horse, a blanket around his shoulders, was Jake Carmmody.

Oh no! Would he tell?

Danny reached the group and dismounted just as Jake walked up. He gave her a long, appraising look. She was in for it now.

But instead of saying anything, Jake just handed Pa the blanket. Then he wheeled his horse and started toward Home Station. Just before he left the station yard, he hesitated. Then he turned back, raised his hand, and gave Danny a quick salute. ●

Based on what you have read, do you think you would be a good Pony Express rider? Why or why not?

# THE PONY EXPRESS

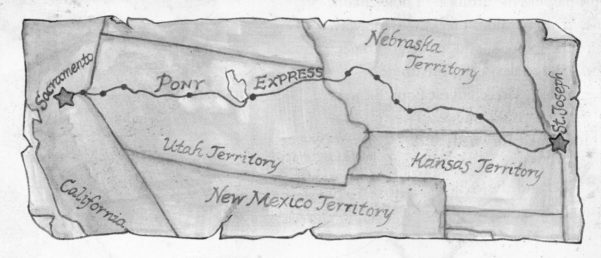

The Pony Express delivered mail from St. Joseph, Missouri, to Sacramento, California—a route of 1,966 miles. The company that organized it was trying to win a contract to deliver the U.S. mail.

Riders changed horses every 10 or 15 miles at way stations and continued for 55 to 120 miles, depending upon the roughness of the terrain. They were expected to switch horses in 2 minutes or less.

Many of the Express horses were wild mustangs, recently caught. A few had never before been ridden when the riders swung up onto their backs.

Riders for the Pony Express waded through 20-foot snowdrifts, climbed mountains, and swam flooded streams— all for $25 per week. On the very first run, a horse got swept away in a Nebraska river and the rider had to borrow a new mount from a bystander.

It took at least 23 days to reach the West Coast by stagecoach; the Pony Express set a record of 7 days and 17 hours, delivering President Lincoln's Gettysburg Address.

The Pony Express was very popular. People gathered to watch the riders and plucked hair from horses' tails for souvenirs. Sometimes they tried to grab bits of clothing from the riders, too!

The Overland Pony Express lasted for only a year and a half, from April 1860, to October 1861. It was put out of business by the newly invented telegraph machine.

Historians say the Pony Express helped our nation stay together by uniting the West with the rest of the country during the time of the Civil War.

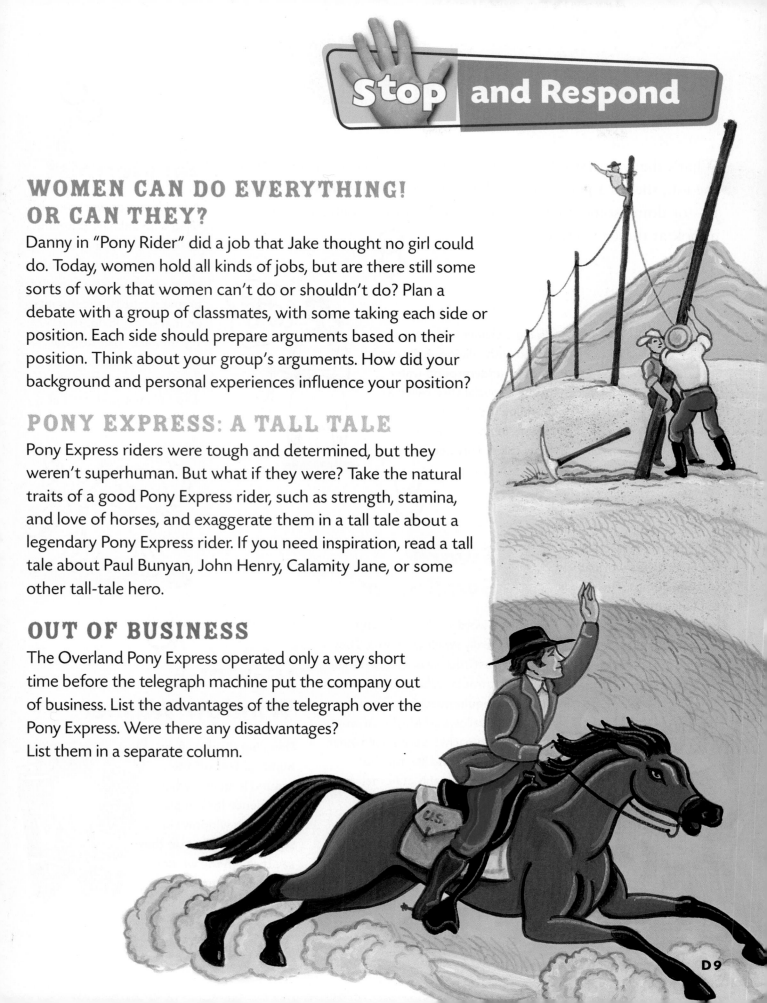

## WOMEN CAN DO EVERYTHING! OR CAN THEY?

Danny in "Pony Rider" did a job that Jake thought no girl could do. Today, women hold all kinds of jobs, but are there still some sorts of work that women can't do or shouldn't do? Plan a debate with a group of classmates, with some taking each side or position. Each side should prepare arguments based on their position. Think about your group's arguments. How did your background and personal experiences influence your position?

## PONY EXPRESS: A TALL TALE

Pony Express riders were tough and determined, but they weren't superhuman. But what if they were? Take the natural traits of a good Pony Express rider, such as strength, stamina, and love of horses, and exaggerate them in a tall tale about a legendary Pony Express rider. If you need inspiration, read a tall tale about Paul Bunyan, John Henry, Calamity Jane, or some other tall-tale hero.

## OUT OF BUSINESS

The Overland Pony Express operated only a very short time before the telegraph machine put the company out of business. List the advantages of the telegraph over the Pony Express. Were there any disadvantages? List them in a separate column.

# ODD JOBS

What's the weirdest job you can imagine? No matter how strange the job, there's a good chance that someone, somewhere is doing it—or doing something even stranger. You don't believe it? Take a look at these examples.

## Taxidermist

A taxidermist's workshop is filled with animals. But none of them are barking, snarling, or yelping because none of them are alive. A taxidermist prepares, stuffs, and mounts animal skins. Taxidermists try to make their displays so lifelike that the stuffed animals seem ready to leap off their pedestals at any moment.

## Diviner

Being a diviner has nothing to do with religion. A diviner locates underground water using a special stick called a divining rod. A person who wants to have a well dug may call in a diviner for help.

## Garbage Diver

This job title tells it all. Garbage divers work at garbage dumps. Their job is to plunge into the rotten garbage to clean and repair the pipes that are sunk deep in the trash to release gases.

## Sword Swallower

Sword swallowers don't really swallow swords. They just stick swords down their throats. What's the main requirement for sword swallowing? Maybe an empty stomach! Sword swallowing may sound like fun, but don't try this at home!

## High-Rise Window Washer

Dangling three or four hundred feet off the ground is an everyday experience for people who wash windows in skyscrapers. What do they see through the windows they're washing? We can only guess!

# Robots
## to the Rescue

by Elaine Israel

Robbie the dog doesn't need to be walked, fed, taken to the vet, or even hugged. For some people, Robbie is the perfect pet. That's because Robbie is a *robot* dog. When it was first introduced in the fall of 2000, this deluxe high-tech beast cost $2,500. Since then, other less costly electronic pets have become available. They are so popular that stores keep selling out of them.

Robots have become part of our lives in ways both ordinary and extraordinary. Robots work in factories where they do everything from painting cars to making cookies. Robots help police departments search for and defuse explosives. Robots go where even the bravest

It looks like a dog and walks like a dog. But what does a real dog think of a robot dog?

human intelligence. All robots can move or work with objects. Yet robots don't have emotions; they can't feel happiness, anger, or pain. Robots are said to show no facial expressions, but the proud owners of robot dogs may give you an argument about that.

Based on what you have read so far, what inferences can you make about other work that robots could do?

undersea diver can't go—to examine and photograph wrecked ships and submarines on the bottom of the ocean.

Because robots handle duties that are dangerous for humans, such as those involving explosives and deep-sea exploration, they actually help save lives. Robots as workers also have another advantage— they don't complain. They do work that can be mind-numbing for humans. After all, placing together two parts of a cookie, day in and day out, would be incredibly boring for a human being. But such routine work doesn't matter to robots. That's another robotic benefit: Humans who would ordinarily do boring tasks are freed to work on other, more interesting jobs.

What is a robot? The word *robot* comes from *robata*, which means "work" in Czechoslovakian, an Eastern European language. Some robots can be described as machines that look like human beings and can walk or talk. Some robots are simply stumpy little computers. They, too, operate with what seems to be almost

**Above:** A robotic assembly line in a car manufacturing plant.

**Below:** Robotic or real? You decide!

Robots wouldn't be possible without computers. But the idea of robots has been around for a long time. Leonardo da Vinci, an artist and inventor, made plans for a mechanical man in 1495. Ancient Hebrew folklore mentions an artificial human called a *golem* that could perform tasks. In the 1920s, a stage play told of robots trained to fight in wars turning on their human masters and taking over the world. Science fiction has often included sinister, even evil, machines. But movies have shown another, more endearing, side to robots. Since the early days of movie history, robotlike characters have often been audience favorites. Any fan of *Star Wars, Lost in Space,* and *Short Circuit* can tell you that.

Many people are intrigued by robotics, and it is becoming a very popular hobby. Kits for

building robots have become more available and less costly. As a result, it's not surprising to find ordinary people building robots, often in their garages and living rooms. The Seattle (Washington) Robotics Society, for example, has more than 500 members. Many assemble robots with their children. Whether they are in kindergarten or high school, kids find robots fascinating.

Once you build a robot, what can you do with it? Well, you *could* have it compete at the Robot Games. Officially called the Annual Robot Exhibitions and Sumo Competitions, the games are modeled on the human Olympics. At the Robot Games, however, track-and-field is replaced by a maze from which robots have to escape. Sumo wrestling is a major event, too. No, not between people— between robots! They try to push each other out of a ring. There's even a kind of robotic talent show that you have to see to believe! The games are held toward the end of every summer at the Exploratorium, a science museum in San Francisco, California. Kids are invited to build their own machines and show them to an audience.

But enough of fun and games. Let's return to the serious side of robots. Robots are becoming more and more important in hospital operating rooms and in outer space.

Two hand-made robots fight it out at a robotic wrestling championship.

Doctors are testing the use of a three-armed robot during open-heart surgery. The robot stands at the operating table. A doctor sits at a computer, controlling the robot's arms. The arms hold tiny cameras that take three-dimensional photographs of the heart. The photos are then used to guide the surgeon. The robot also holds very small surgical tools, such as scissors and graspers. The robot helps doctors repair a patient's heart valves through three cuts that are each only one inch long. In regular heart operations, the incisions are longer, so there is a greater chance of infection following surgery. Spokespeople at a hospital where robotic surgery has been performed say that it also has fewer complications than regular surgery. The patient feels less pain afterward, the hospital stay is shorter, and the entire procedure costs much less.

The U.S. Food and Drug Administration (FDA) has approved the use of robots for general surgery but not yet for heart operations. Robotic heart surgery is still experimental. It needs FDA approval before it can be widely used. Many heart surgeons expect that to happen by 2005.

One day very soon, robots may even help to perform surgery in space. Suppose an astronaut aboard the International Space Station has a burst appendix. Not many doctors make house calls these days—and that would be quite a house call! So it must be Dr. Robot to the rescue. The robot could be sent into space. Upon its arrival at the station, surgeons on Earth could tell it what to do.

Based on what you have read, would you want to have a robot perform surgery on you? Why or why not?

NASA, the U.S. space agency, uses robots frequently. NASA plans six robotic missions to Mars by 2015. The robotic spacecraft will search for evidence of life on the red planet.

In 1999, two of NASA's robotic craft, the *Mars Polar Lander* and the *Mars Climate Orbiter,* were lost in space. For upcoming missions, NASA is taking no chances. The new craft will be able to sense almost exactly where to land on Mars. The robot rovers will be programmed to stay away from dangerous objects.

Robots performing operations—really! Robots on Mars—fact, not fiction! We're all used to the wonders of technology. But these are incredible ideas, aren't they? And we are only in the early days of our relationships with robots. Given the advances in robotics, who can tell what the future will bring?

NASA plans to send robotic spacecraft like these to Mars.

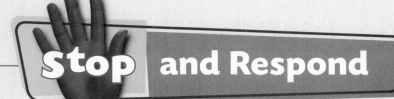

# Stop and Respond

## Robots I Have Known

What robots have you read about or seen on television or in the movies? Discuss robot characters with a partner or a small group of classmates. Are there certain robots that everyone remembers? Why are those characters memorable? Compare the inferences you've made about robots with the others in your group. How did your inferences differ? What do you think influenced each person's inferences?

## Design a Robot

Design your own personal robot. Draw a picture of your robot, write its name, and label its important parts. Then describe the purpose and special features of your robot.

## Human or Robot?

There's something a bit strange about the new neighbor down the block, but you can't pinpoint exactly what it is. Could your new neighbor be some kind of robot? Use this idea to write a story or poem.

# The Drummer Boy of Chickamauga

Can you imagine fighting in a war at the age of fourteen, twelve, or even ten? Many thousands of young men fought in the Civil War. Most of the boys younger than thirteen were musicians who played the fife, the bugle, or the drums. Drummers rode into battle with the rest of the troops, signaling the start of battle or a retreat.

The most famous of the drummer boys on the Union side was Johnny Clem, the "Drummer Boy of Chickamauga." John Lincoln Clem ran away from his home in Newark, Ohio, to join the army in 1861. He was not yet ten years old. Johnny tagged along after Company C of the twenty-second Michigan Volunteer Infantry as an unofficial drummer boy. The officers chipped in for his soldier's salary—$13 a month.

At Shiloh in 1862, Clem's drum was smashed by weapon fire. A year later at the Battle of Chickamauga, he rode into battle on a cannon, carrying a musket shortened to fit his size. A Confederate colonel chased after him, shouting. Clem shot and killed the colonel. That's how Clem gained national attention as the "Drummer Boy of Chickamauga." He was later promoted to the rank of sergeant.

Johnny Clem stayed with the army throughout the war. He retired from the army as a major general in 1915. Clem died in 1937 and is buried at Arlington National Cemetery.

## INFERRING

# Crime in the Cubicle

Compare the **inferences** Shanti made as she read the passage from *Crime in the Cubicle* with the ones you made as you read the same words.

> Anna is really brave. If she were a real person, I'd like to meet her.

> Being stubborn is a good quality to have if you're trying to solve a mystery. I'm stubborn myself.

As Anna tiptoed into the cubicle, she heard a soft, rustling sound. *I'm so nervous, I'm hearing things,* she thought to herself. *I know everyone is downstairs at the office party. I saw them all there.* Anna hated going anywhere near this cubicle. It was the one her pal John had entered and from which he had disappeared. But Anna was being her usual stubborn self and wasn't about to give up until she figured out what happened to her friend . . .

> I'll bet there's someone hiding in the cubicle.

> With so many people in one place, somebody could easily have sneaked away without Anna noticing.

> I'm sure Anna will eventually figure out the mystery. I've never read a book that ended with the mystery unsolved.

Think about the many kinds of inferences you make as you read. You draw conclusions as you collect information from the text. You make inferences when you use that information to make predictions about what will happen next. The important thing in making an inference is to use the text as a starting point but to go *beyond* the words on the page to better understand what you are reading. Try to think about what the author is trying to tell you that *isn't directly stated.* Have a continual mental conversation with the author as you use the text and your own knowledge and experience to solve your own reading "mysteries."

# Lemonade for Sale

### by Beth Raisner Glass

"You squeeze the lemons, and I'll pour the water," instructed James as he wiped the sweat from his brow. The bright morning sun was already baking James and Allie's lemonade stand, promising a brilliant and prosperous day.

"Oo-oo-oo, James," squealed Allie, her lips puckering, "something's not quite right! It's so sour!"

"We forgot the sugar, that's why," answered James, reaching into the bucket. "Two scoops and we'll be ready for business."

James and Allie took turns

stirring the lemonade and setting plastic cups on the table of their freshly-painted lemonade stand. The lemon juice mixed with the sugar gave the liquid a cloudy appearance.

"Do you think we're charging enough? Twenty-five cents a cup seems cheap. It'll take *forever* to earn enough money to buy Mom and Dad's anniversary present," complained James.

Allie just shrugged. Being a year younger, she'd grown accustomed to letting her ten-year-old brother make all the money decisions. But then an idea came to her. "James, why don't we charge twenty-five cents for the lemonade and five cents for the cup? That way, we can earn a little extra money on each sale!" Allie was on a roll and continued, "And then we could sell the ice and the—"

"Hold on, Allie . . . is that legal?" asked James.

Blowing her bangs off her sweaty forehead, Allie considered the question. "Yes," Allie answered decisively. "I do believe it is."

With that decision made, James and Allie began their sale. People crowded around the stand in no time. James and Allie worked together—one did the pouring and the other piled up the collection of coins.

Peering from the family room windows, their parents stood watching and smiling as the crowd filled the street. Their parents had approved their plans for their lemonade sale and even helped them with their preparations.

"We'll take two glasses, please!" called Michael and Laurie, the twins from down the street.

"I'll have three! I'm so dry from all this heat!" ordered Ms. Tepper, who ran in any weather.

"It certainly *is* hot today," said Joe. "I'll take one with extra ice, please!" Allie smelled the sweet, freshly-cut grass wafting over from Joe's house next door and smiled as she scooped out the extra ice cubes.

> Do you think James and Allie's lemonade sale will be successful? What information in the text leads you to this conclusion?

Good Job!   **D 19**

# Trinkets to Treasures

As the day wore on, James and Allie were nearing their goal. James's face glowed as he exclaimed, "I have to admit that this is turning out better than I ever thought it would." Then he studied the scene in front of him. All the cups were gone, the lemonade pitcher had been emptied four times, and the napkins were sold out. All that was left of the ice was a puddle. Even the lemonade stand itself was sold to the highest bidder. "We have nothing left to sell!" Allie laughed.

"Allie," said James, "if we made this much money selling lemonade today, just think how much money we could make if we sold other things . . . like stuff from the house!" A slow smile spread over Allie's face. Springing into action, the two darted for the house.

By four o'clock, James and Allie had set up a new kind of stand. "Trinkets to Treasures" read the new sign. While their parents were busy inside, Allie brought out a football and a telephone and sold them for five dollars each. James found a fishing rod and a small television. He sold each of those for eight dollars. A teapot and candlesticks— "collectors' specials"— sold for six dollars each. Before they knew it, James and Allie had acquired a small fortune. But before long, a gloomy sky forced the sale to end. Neighbors started to walk home with their trinkets and treasures and waved to a proud James and Allie.

How do you think James and Allie's parents will react to this new sale? What information in the text and your own experience leads you to believe this?

Just then, their mother glanced out the window. Taken aback by the scene outside, she cried out, "What . . . ? There's my teapot . . . and our television, too! What is Mrs. Clayton doing with them?"

"Hey!" called James and Allie's confused father. "What in the world is Mr. Lyons doing with my bamboo fly-fishing rod—and my baseball card collection? I've had that since I was eight years old!"

"What about my best running shoes? I ran a marathon in those!" cried Mom in a state of panic.

They hurried out to the driveway and confronted their children. Allie and James stood frozen in front of their parents.

"Now, if I remember correctly," said their father, "you two were supposed to have a *lemonade* sale. That means lemons, water, sugar, and ice."

"Minus the television, teapot, running shoes, and baseball card collection," explained their mother. She gulped when she saw her grandmother's cedar hope chest with a price tag of four dollars taped to it. As Mom tried to figure out what had happened, she thought about the best way to get their things back without ruining her children's enthusiasm.

Their parent's reaction, however, had already dampened James and Allie's good mood. After all, their goal had been to make money to buy an anniversary present for their parents. They had simply gotten caught up in the excitement of the sale.

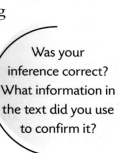

Was your inference correct? What information in the text did you use to confirm it?

"Mom, Dad," James began, "I guess Allie and I went a bit overboard. We were just so excited to make money. But I guess I'd be upset, too, if someone sold all my favorite things. We'll figure out a way to get your stuff back," James promised.

A look passed between Mom and Dad. They agreed to let James and Allie try to solve the problem on their own. So James and Allie were left alone to clean up and think of a new plan. They packed up the "Trinkets to Treasures" sign and the rest of the household items that were on the lawn before heading toward the kitchen. While looking for a snack to re-energize them, James had another inspiration.

What do you think James and Allie might do now? Why do you think so?

Sold

"I've got it!" James cried. "We have to go door-to-door to give all the money back."

"And get Mom and Dad's stuff back," Allie reminded her brother.

"Yes, of course, and get Mom and Dad's stuff back," he continued. "We'll have to apologize. And what better way is there to apologize to everyone than with a plate of cookies? We'll make them ourselves!"

Allie smiled and licked her lips. "I like this plan already."

The next day was as hot as the last. The sun broke through the clouds and burned them away by early morning. Allie and James, pulling their old wagon, went to each neighbor's door, collecting items, returning money, and delivering cookies.

Was your inference correct? If not, reread the last paragraph on page D21 to look for any clues you might have missed.

"These are the best cookies I've ever had!" said Ms. Tepper.

"Did you make these? They're fantastic!" said the twins' parents.

"How can I get my hands on more of these tasty cookies?" asked Joe.

James and Allie smiled at each other. By noon, they had run back to their house and straight for the kitchen.

"I'll make the sign!" declared Allie, getting her cash box ready.

"And I'll make the cookies!" said James, with a spatula in one hand and a bag of chocolate chips in the other. "It looks like we're back in business!" ⬤

# Stop and Respond

## The Name Game

James and Allie called their new stand "Trinkets to Treasures." From that name, what inferences can you make about what they are selling? Think up four or five other good names for James and Allie's business. Then read your list to a friend. Underline the name your friend prefers and the name you like best. If it's the same name, make two lines under it.

## Kids at Work

Brainstorm with one or several classmates good ways kids who are too young to have regular jobs can make money. Jot down some of your favorite ideas. Then compare your list with another group's list. Which ideas seem like sure-fire winners?

## Think Again!

James had a really bad idea—selling their parents' belongings—and Allie went along with it. Sometimes it's not easy to say no to someone who wants you to do something you know you shouldn't. What advice would you give about listening to your conscience and standing up for what you know is right?

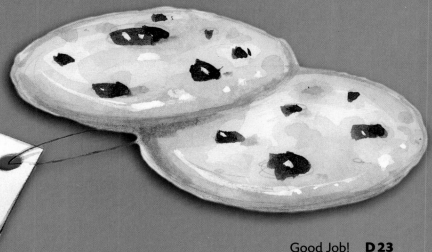

$1.00

# The WHO and Even the OOPS!

BY LISA PALAZZOLO

Many ordinary inventions have an extraordinary history. These true stories about the inventors and some mistakes behind the inventions we now use every day include an exploding egg, shattered china, spilled ink, and more. These are tales of the struggles of people just like you and me who tried to find inventive ways to solve problems.

## Inventions in the Kitchen

Josephine Cochrane invented the dishwasher in 1886, but not because she hated washing dishes. This wealthy American enjoyed hosting elegant dinner parties that showed off her fine china. But the servants cringed whenever a dinner party was scheduled. They knew they would have to spend hours washing the delicate porcelain and listening to Cochrane rant every time a piece was accidentally broken.

One night, upset over the sound of shattering china plates, Cochrane cried out, "If nobody else is going to invent a dishwashing machine, I'll do it myself!"

It was a challenging task, but Cochrane was determined to succeed. After breaking a few dishes herself, she finally patented the "Cochrane Dishwasher" in 1886. Her invention, which rinsed dishes safely in hot, soapy water, won first prize at the 1893 Chicago World's Fair, and businessmen rushed to install it in their hotels and restaurants. It became a household appliance by the 1950s.

No one actually invented microwaves. Microwave energy happens naturally as electricity travels through a conductor. But the idea of using microwave energy for cooking was discovered accidentally by another American in 1946.

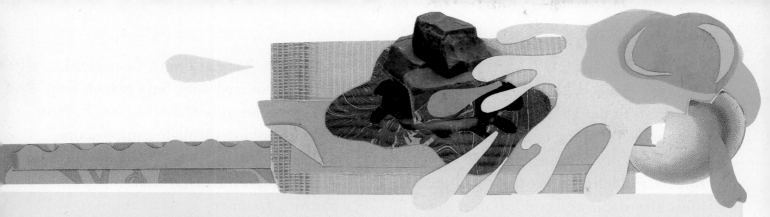

Percy Spencer had taught himself everything he needed to know about being a scientist. One day, while testing a piece of electrical equipment in his laboratory, Spencer reached for a chocolate bar. He found that it had melted and wondered why. Curious, he put popcorn kernels near the energy source and was surprised when they popped. Calling another scientist over, Spencer put an unshelled egg in the same place. The egg shook as its temperature rose, and Spencer's friend got splattered as the eggshell burst!

Spencer knew that a gas range cooked well, but microwave energy would cook even better. It could cook foods faster and save people time. Spencer began experimenting and invented the microwave oven. But it was over 5 feet tall and weighed about 750 pounds! Since it was too big for use in homes, Spencer's company sold it to hospitals and restaurants. Once its size was adjusted, the microwave oven was adapted for home use. By the 1970s, more American homes had a microwave oven than a dishwasher.

Like the dishwasher and the microwave oven, it took a while for the can and the can opener to become

> Based on what you have read so far, what qualities do you think would be important for an inventor to have?

household items. Putting food into a sealed tin can to keep it fresh was the idea of English businessman Peter Durand in 1810. Sailors, explorers, and soldiers could now enjoy fresh, prepared foods even though they were far from home. But opening cans was dangerous. People used any sharp, metal object to open a can, and they often got injured. In 1858, American inventor Ezra Warner decided to make a better can opener. His design had a sharp metal point for forcing into the lid, but people often punctured their hands as well as the cans themselves. Only American soldiers on the Civil War battlefield would use it. Determined to make can-opening safer and easier, William Lyman, an American, made a can opener with two handles and a cutting wheel. Patented in 1870, Lyman's design worked very well.

# Closet Inventions

Jacob Davis, a Nevada tailor, created blue jeans in the 1870s. His work pants were made of strong cotton denim, dyed dark blue to hide stains, and had metal zippers and buttons. People found the blue jeans affordable and comfortable. But as the fabric softened, it ripped. Davis then made his clothing more durable by adding metal rivets to the places where they tore.

Since Davis could not afford to patent his idea, he contacted San Francisco businessman Levi Strauss. The two began selling blue jeans and became an overnight success. More than 100 years later, jeans are worn by people everywhere. In some countries, new jeans can be used as money!

Zippers were not invented for blue jeans, but instead, as fasteners for shoes. Buttons did not work, and shoes kept falling off people's feet. In 1893, a metal fastener named the "Clasp Locker" was invented by W. Judson, a clothing manufacturer. But it was a failure. So Judson's son-in-law, G. Sundback, invented the "Separable Fastener" in 1917. Heavier, with more teeth, it kept shoes securely in place. When a tire and rubber company needed a fastener for rubber boots, they used Sundback's design, calling it a *zipper* for the ZZZZZZZZIP sound it made.

Instead of zippers, your shoes may be fastened with a kind of hook and loop tape. One day in the late 1940s, a mountain climber named George de Mestral and his dog were hiking through the Swiss countryside. Back at home, he noticed they were covered with burs, which help seeds travel because they cling to clothing and fur. Looking through a microscope, de Mestral saw the burs had many little hooks and got the inspiration to make a clothing fastener.

In early 1948, de Mestral began experimenting with different fabrics, trying to create little hooks. Nothing worked, and people laughed at his continued failure. But de Mestrel did not quit. By 1955, he had discovered that nylon forms little hooks when heated. He used this discovery to invent a successful clothing fastener. He named it by combining two French words meaning *velvet* and *small hooks*. Today, velcro® fasteners are used worldwide and even in outer space to keep astronauts' space suits closed.

> Have you confirmed or changed your earlier inference about the qualities inventors need? What information in the text did you use do this?

# Inventions for Play

The search for a fun and inexpensive means of transportation led to the invention of the bicycle. The first bicycle, created in France in about 1790, did not have handlebars or pedals. Riders pushed their way along, leaning from side to side to steer. In 1817, German inventor von Drais invented the *draisienne,* a bicycle with handlebars. Twenty-two years later, Scottish blacksmith K. Macmillan added pedals.

By 1860, the bicycle had undergone even more changes. It became known as the *velocipede,* a name which comes from two Latin words meaning *rapid* and *foot.* The velocipede helped people travel faster because one rotation of its pedals meant one rotation of its great front wheel. Less effort was now required to cycle, but the new design had its drawbacks. Since the front wheel was 5 feet in diameter, the seat was high in the air and accidents resulted in serious injury. Its metal wheels earned it the nickname "boneshaker"—the faster the ride,

the more uncomfortable the rider. By the early 1900s, small rubber tires, gears, and handbrakes made for a safer ride.

Another popular toy came from a baking company. From 1871 to 1958, this company sold a lot of pies to New England colleges. Each pie came in an aluminum pie plate, and college students enjoyed tossing the empty metal discs around campus. Playing with aluminum pie plates was great fun, but the discs could not fly once they were bent. Also, the sharp metal edges could injure players. To solve the problem, two American soldiers returning from World War II, F. Morrison and W. Franscioni, invented a disc made of a mixture of wood and resin. It could hold up under ordinary wear, but it shattered on impact. Finally, the two men made one from plastic. Today you can choose from a variety of plain or fancy plastic flying discs.

# Desktop Inventions

In prehistoric times, people scratched pictures into the walls of caves by using sharpened stones. Ancient civilizations used bone, ivory, and metal to put marks on stone or clay tablets. By the year 400 A.D., a permanent ink—which included the juice of berries and bark mixed with iron— was invented in Europe. For over a thousand years, people poured ink into the hollow center of a feather and wrote. These *quills* worked, but they broke easily and were messy.

Many types of pens were invented through the years, but the most successful one was patented by American L. E. Waterman in 1884. An insurance agent, Waterman became frustrated when he spilled ink all over an important contract. Waterman's "fountain pen" did not leak, but the ink still smeared.

In 1938, Hungarian journalist L. Biro noticed that the thick ink used to print newspapers did not smudge, but he could not get it to flow through a fountain pen. So he created the ballpoint pen, which allowed the ink to flow onto a rotating steel ball. This pen became a success during World War II when fighter plane pilots discovered that a ballpoint pen would not leak at high altitudes like fountain pens did.

When rubber was imported to Europe from South American rain forests, people discovered that small pieces of it could rub out pencil marks. That is how rubber got its name: it "rubbed out" mistakes. But rubber, because it is a natural material, rots quickly. To make erasers last longer, Charles Goodyear invented the process of "vulcanization." This word comes from the name of the Roman god of fire, Vulcan. Goods made from heated rubber last longer.

From what you read in this article, do you think you could be an inventor? Why or why not?

Familiar household items such as the dishwasher, the bicycle, and the ballpoint pen may not come to mind when people think of inventions. But these accomplishments are still remarkable, the result of dedication and creative problem solving. We use these everyday objects . . . well . . . every day, and our lives are better because of them. Now what problem would *you* like to solve?

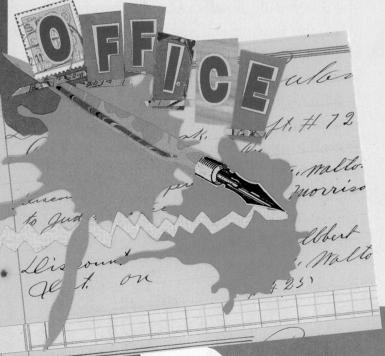

## Inventions of the Future

Were you inspired by the accounts of the inventions you read about? Get together with a few classmates to dream up some inventions of your own. Perhaps your inventions will solve problems or will just make life in the future easier. Draw pictures of your inventions and write about the work they do.

## It's the Greatest!

In this article, you have read about inventions that make people's everyday lives easier. Based on what you've read and what is important to you, which everyday invention is it hardest for you to imagine doing without? Why? Describe your favorite invention and explain why it is so important to you.

## Did You Know?

Choose one of the inventions you read about in "The 'Who' and Even the 'Oops!'" Learn more details about the invention on the Internet or from books or magazine articles. Perhaps you'll discover early versions of the invention that didn't work very well. Maybe you'll read about forgotten inventions that tried to solve the same problem as the successful one. Make a poster or chart to share what you learn with the rest of the class.

## Let's Write

### Talking About Work

Interview an adult about his or her job. Prepare for the interview by reading about the work the person does so you can ask good questions. Make sure you arrive on time for the interview well supplied with pens, paper, and audiotapes if you plan to record the interview. Write up the interview for the classroom or school newspaper. Remember to send the person you interviewed a copy of the interview along with a thank-you letter.

### Good Jobs

Turn to the classified ad section of a newspaper and find the employment ads. What information is included in a typical job ad? Write an advertisement for a job of your choice. Make sure that the ad is eye-catching, describes the job clearly, includes the qualifications for the job, and tells where to send applications.

### Work Rules

What qualities do good employers have? What makes good employees? Write a list of rules for good bosses and a list of rules for good workers. Are any of the rules the same?

### Do School and Work Mix?

Do you think high school students should hold after-school jobs? Talk to some high school students to find out what they think. Then write a persuasive paper in which you argue for or against high school students working after school.

## More Books

Barkin, Carol and Elizabeth James. *Jobs for Kids.* Lothrop, Lee, & Shepherd, 1990.

Jones, Vada Lee. *Kids Can Make Money, Too.* Calico Paws, 1987.

Kroll, Steven. *Pony Express!* Scholastic, 1996.

Murphy, Jim. *Weird and Wacky Inventions.* Crown, 1978.

Saller, Carol. *Working Children.* Carolrhoda, 1998.

Turvey, Peter. *Inventions: Inventors and Ingenious Ideas.* F. Watts, 1992.

Walsh, Jill Paton. *A Chance Child.* Farrar, Straus, and Giroux, 1978.

## On the Web

**Pony Express**
http://www.xphomestation.com

**Jobs**
http://www.talentedkids.com/jobs/jobs.php

**Inventions**
http://www.inventors.about.com/
science/inventors/cs/famousinventions/
index.htm
http://www.cbc4kids.ca/general/the-lab/
history-of-invention/default.html

## Across the Curriculum

### Science/Health

Check Web sites and magazine and newspaper articles to learn about some of the latest and most amazing inventions in health care. Try to find information about any of the new medical procedures that use robotics. Choose one of the new medical procedures you've read about and describe it to your classmates. Use visual aids—photos, diagrams, sketches—to help you explain the procedure.

### Art

Make a three-dimensional model of a robot. You can make your robot look like a human being or anything else you like. Be prepared to explain what your robot is designed to do and how its features help it accomplish that task.

# Volunteering: What a Great Job!

**"We make a living by what we get. We make a life by what we give."**
—Sir Winston Churchill

Volunteering is one of the best ways you can spend time. Think about it! You can take pride in helping to make the world a better place as you learn new skills and meet new friends.

Are you concerned about the environment? Work with other people to clean up a park or organize a recycling program. Do you like animals? Volunteer at a zoo or animal shelter. Or bring your pet to visit people at a nursing home or hospital. Thinking about becoming a teacher? Tutor a younger student who's having trouble with math or reading.

Did you know that various groups organize once-a-year service days? You can find out about two of them—Make a Difference Day and National Youth Service Day—on the Internet. You can find Web sites for such organizations as Servenet, America's Promise, and the Hungersite.

National organizations such as the National Audubon Society and the World Wildlife Federation have local youth programs you may want to find out about. Or you can choose among youth service clubs such as Boy Scouts and Girl Scouts, Campfire Boy's and Girl's Clubs, and 4-H Clubs. And there are religious groups, neighborhood teams, and family organizations. The list is nearly endless, but the important thing is to make a start and start volunteering. It's a great job!